HAIL
TO THE
CHIEFS

ALSO BY BARBARA HOLLAND

SECRETS OF THE CAT

HAIL
TO THE
CHIEFS

★ ★ ★

Barbara Holland

*How to Tell Your Polks
from Your Tylers*

BALLANTINE BOOKS
New York

Library of Congress Catalog Card Number: 89-91495

ISBN: 0-345-36273-X

Cover design by William Geller
Text design by Mary A. Wirth

Manufactured in the United States of America
First Edition: June 1990
10 9 8 7 6 5 4 3 2

To My Mother

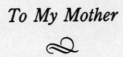

Table of Contents

Introduction

The trouble with American History is that you don't remember it, and why should you? Nobody does. American History is what we had to trudge through before we could get on to the good stuff: Mary Queen of Scots, Nero, Catherine the Great, Attila the Hun, Marie Antoinette, Vikings, pharaohs, and the Great Plague. It was prerequisite to everything exciting, and it consisted entirely of stout, middle-aged men in waistcoats and muttonchop whiskers who only thought about tariffs. Oh, sometimes they took a break from tariffs and thought about the Federal Reserve Bank or the Gold Standard for a while, but then they always brushed the cigar ash off their tummies and went back to tariffs again.

No American President ever smothered his nephews in the Tower or clutched an asp to his bosom, and if they ever did anything but sit there in the Oval Office stroking their whiskers and thinking about money, our history books didn't mention it. It would have been disrespectful. That's why they stuck to tariffs; none of us woke up long enough to disrespect a tariff.

The following pages contain everything you're likely to remember or want to know about American History. After all, you've already had one chance to remember the McKinley Tariff and Van Buren's Vice-President, and you muffed it. No point in reminding you now. However, after you finish this book, you will know enough Memorable Things about the Presidents to impress your fellow guests at the average dinner party. People may even be so awed they'll assume you know all about tariffs, too, but don't worry; they won't ask. *Nobody* wants to know about tariffs.

HAIL
TO THE
CHIEFS

George Washington

1789–1797

★

ou're wrong about George Washington. Nathaniel Hawthorne was wrong too. He said, "He had no nakedness, but was born with clothes on, and his hair powdered, and made a stately bow on his first appearance in the world."[1] People rarely feel all warm and cozy about Washington. They look at pictures of his wife and think he must have been a stranger to the tender passion, and maybe the birds and the bees do it but George didn't.

To all this I say, Then what about Sally Fairfax?

As a young country colonel, George fell in love with several pretty girls who wouldn't marry him.[2] Then he met Sally. She was said to be a bit of a flirt, and had excellent connections. However, she was married to a friend of his. In the evenings George hung around Belvoir, the Fairfax place, dancing[3] and playing cards and staring at Sally until the Fairfaxes got quite cross. Even when he was off soldiering, he couldn't stop thinking about her and wrote her such friendly letters that her relatives felt obliged to complain. Just before he married Martha he wrote to Sally promising lifelong devotion, and the year before he died, when she was sixty-eight, he wrote saying that nothing in his career "had been able to eradicate from my mind those happy moments, the happiest of my life, which I have enjoyed in your company."

So there.

Martha was short and dumpy and had more than the usual number of chins, but she was pleasant enough. (Her grandson said she had nice eyes.) By an odd coincidence, she was also the richest widow in Virginia. She liked to putter around

---

[1] Hawthorne wasn't born till 1804, so what would he know?

[2] There was talk about a Mary Phillipse, heiress to enormous tracts of land along the Hudson. George always felt enormous tracts of land gave a girl a certain something.

[3] He still had his own teeth.

the kitchen lifting the lids off the kettles and tasting things, and helping the slaves fix George's favorite dinner—cream of peanut soup, Smithfield ham with oyster sauce, mashed sweet potatoes with coconut, string beans with mushrooms, spoonbread, and whiskey cake. (See Appendix I.)

As First Lady, she gave rather stiff parties that ended sharp at nine o'clock,[4] when she blew out the candles and she and George went to bed, guests or no guests. By all reports they grew quite fond of each other. I can't imagine why they weren't blessed with issue.

In the beginning, George Washington was born in a house with a chimney at each end, halfway between Pope's and Bridge's creeks, and he was scared of his mother. Everyone was. She was a vindictive woman with a savage temper, and all her children left home just as fast as possible. She refused to go to George's inauguration and said terrible things about him every chance she got.[5]

When George was eleven his father died. I hope you've forgotten the cherry tree story. It was invented by Parson Weems in 1800, and the moral—that you can commit any outrage you like as long as you confess to it afterward—has misled generations of Americans.[6] Most people believed the whole book. Most people will believe anything.

We don't know any true stories about his boyhood because he didn't tell us any.[7] IIe did write a letter to Richard Henry Lee when they were both nine, thanking him for a book with pictures of elephants. He claimed he could "read

---

[4] It seemed later.

[5] Once he took her to a ball in Fredericksburg, but she wore such horrible old clothes that everyone was embarrassed. She did it on purpose.

[6] Weems made up a lot of other pious Washingtoniana too. Do you want to hear the one about God and the flower bed? Why not?

[7] He was trying to forget.

3 or 4 pages sometimes without missing a word," and added that if it didn't rain his mother might let him ride his pony, Hero, over for a visit. (I realize this isn't very exciting stuff but it's all I could find. I suppose you think you could come up with something better.)

He never went to college, or learned any Latin or Greek or got too much further than the book about elephants. In later life he had a nice library with lots of books like *Diseases of Horses, A Treatise on Peat Moss,* and *Mease on the Bite of a Mad Dog,* but basically he was a man of action.

At fourteen he tried to run away to sea, but his mother stopped him, and then when he was sixteen his half brother got him a job surveying for the Fairfaxes,[8] and so for several years he trudged around measuring the boondocks and rejoicing at getting away from Mother.

When he was twenty-one, Virginia was having some problems with France, and George got commissioned a lieutenant colonel in the militia. He rushed right out and attacked a French scouting party, which was silly, and accidentally started the French and Indian War. People forgave him, though, after Braddock's Defeat, which I don't have time to discuss right now. He was never much of a military star, but he was brave enough and always looked good on a horse, and that was the main thing. A strapping lad (one source calls him "a noble youth"), he was six foot three,[9] with size thirteen boots and big heavy fists with which he sometimes forgot himself and knocked unruly soldiers out cold. He'd inherited his mother's temper. From a distance he may have looked like a frozen halibut, but he spent his life grinding his dentures and counting to ten to keep from breaking heads.

---

[8] They were relations, kind of. Lord Fairfax was George's half brother's father-in-law's cousin. He was a great Loyalist, and when he heard George had won the war he dropped dead.

[9] His bed was only six feet long. His feet stuck out.

When he was annoyed his language made his secretary shake in his shoes.

By age twenty-three he was a full colonel, and defended the Virginia borders against the usual French and Indians.[10] When this was over he went home to take care of Mount Vernon, which he'd inherited from his half brother, and things were pretty quiet for a long time, but George didn't mind. He liked farming. First he rode around supervising his slaves for a while, and then he sat on the veranda with a tall cool one.[11] Farming can be fun if you have the right kind of help. Sometimes he sent for his hounds, Vulcan, Truelove, Ringwood, Rockwood, Sweetlips, Singer, Forester, and Music,[12] and he and his neighbors chased foxes until it was time for dinner, which he enjoyed very much, considering.

You'll want to know about his teeth. Everyone asks. Well, before he was fifty he'd lost most of them, though he did hang on to the lower left premolar until he was sixty-five, and his dentures had a hole punched for it to stick through. He was sentimental about it, and why not? For the rest, he tried this and he tried that and nothing seemed to work very well. (President Harding's son wrote an article about it for the *Journal of Oral Surgery.*) One set of dentures had eight human teeth—I don't know whose—screwed in with gold rivets. One set was made with a pound of lead. The set you're thinking of, the one that makes him look so constipated in that Gilbert Stuart portrait, was carved out of hippopotamus ivory and was no good for chewing. It was

---

[10] The results speak for themselves.

[11] He'd pledged never to sell a slave, so naturally he ended up with a surplus. There were over three hundred, way more than he needed, but having a lot of extras lounging around gave a nice tone to the place.

[12] If you go to Virginia today you will find that all hounds are still called Vulcan, Truelove, Ringwood, etc., but they are *not the same hounds.*

just for cosmetic purposes.[13] It was held in place by a kind of spring device wedged into his jaws, but it would have fallen out if he'd smiled. It wouldn't have been fitting for him to smile anyway. Eisenhower was the first military president who smiled, and that was years later.

In 1775, the First Continental Congress fingered him as commander in chief against the British. He hadn't been soldiering in eighteen years and never was any Napoleon,[14] but they wanted him because the war was being held in Massachusetts and they needed a Virginian so the South would take an interest in it.

So Washington buckled on his sword and went off to Boston to win the Revolution. He refused to accept a salary. He said he'd just send bills for his expenses instead. Everyone thought this was pretty darned noble of him, and he was impressed himself and kept dragging it into the conversation afterward, and even mentioned it in his will. The salary he turned down would have come to $48,000; the expenses he billed instead came to $447,220.[15] He did like to set an example of austerity for his starving troops, though, and drank only from a pair of very plain sterling silver goblets with nothing engraved on them but his family crest. His crest is half a duck sitting in a crown, possibly laying an egg, and very nice if you like that kind of thing.

There's a pretty story about him kneeling in prayer in the snow at Valley Forge, and you're welcome to believe it if you want, but he had a famous aversion to kneeling. When Martha dragged him to church on Sundays, he wouldn't kneel at the customary points in the Episcopal service. This made him kind of conspicuous but he didn't care.

---

[13] A man who needs hippopotamus teeth for cosmetic purposes is a desperate man.

[14] Luckily the British were worse.

[15] That included a lot of Madeira. He was fond of Madeira, and needed to keep his strength up.

After the war he went back to Mount Vernon to be enormously famous. People thought he was our national hero,[16] and came from all over the world to make paintings and life masks of him and detailed drawings of everything he wore or ate from or sat on or wrote with during the war. They published miles of poetry calling him "the First of Heroes," "Glory's Deathless Heir," "a second Moses," and other things too embarrassing to repeat.

When he wasn't sitting for portraits, he thought about mules. Mules are the offspring of mares and jackasses, and since we didn't have any jackasses, we couldn't have any mules. Horses are all very well, but sometimes only a mule will fill the bill. The King of Spain sent George an enormous gray jackass named Royal Gift, and Gift meant well but when it came to sex, he couldn't see what all the fuss was about. Then Lafayette sent him a black one named Knight of Malta with "the ferocity of a tiger," and the mule scheme was off and running.

Then in 1789 George was unanimously elected President of the United States and had to leave for New York.[17]

He was a good President because of being our national hero and nobody wanting to make him mad. When the Pennsylvania farmers rose up in the Whiskey Rebellion, all he had to do was go *look* at them and they fell down apologizing.

He kept saying he wanted to go home to Mount Vernon, but we made him serve a second term anyway.

John Adams was his Vice-President, and didn't he just hate it. He called the office "the most insignificant . . . that ever the invention of man contrived."[18]

After eight years, Hamilton and Madison wrote the fa-

---

[16] They hadn't heard about Lincoln yet.

[17] Later they said New York was a sink of political vice and moved the capital to Philadelphia, but that didn't last either.

[18] Either you have the vice-presidential temperament or you don't.

mous "Washington's Farewell Address," and everyone cried. Adams delivered the reply to it, and they cried harder. Some say even Adams cried. Why do I doubt this?

A couple of years later George was riding around Mount Vernon thinking about mules and caught a chill, and by the next morning he had a nasty strep throat. Feeling it urgent to get bled as quickly as possible, he sent for Mr. Rawlins, one of the overseers, to start the job while they waited for Dr. Craik. Martha thought maybe Rawlins shouldn't take quite so *much* blood, but he did. Then Craik arrived and took some more, and tried to make George gargle with vinegar. By eleven he wasn't any better, so Craik bled him again, and at three Dr. Dick was called in and bled him a fourth time, but even that didn't help and George was dead before midnight. (If the last word on his lips was "Sally," it isn't something they'd be likely to tell us about.)

Your history teacher told you Washington freed his slaves in his will, but she was lying. He did free his old valet, William, who was doubtless delighted though totally crippled by this time, but freeing slaves wasn't as simple as it looks from here. It wasn't quite like chopping the shackles off three hundred adult white male CPAs in midtown Manhattan. We're taking a colony of illiterate, semiskilled men, women, and children, with the usual number of them infants, elderly, or helpless, and sending them off to look for work among plantation owners as eager to hire free blacks as mine owners a hundred years later were eager to hire union organizers.

The neighbors would have broken every window in Mount Vernon.

In any case freeing the slaves would have been illegal, since so many of them were either Martha's dower slaves or related to them, and not George's to dispose of.

He did say in his will that when *Martha* died, the slaves that had been George's when they married should be freed, or at least those still young enough to take an interest in freedom. He also left word they should be taught to read and write, and those of suitable age be trained in carpentry or masonry or something so as not to starve to death. He knew a lot more about the local job market than your history teacher.

It would be wrong to leave the subject of our first President without recording Washington's Joke. It seems he was sitting at dinner when the fireplace behind him got too hot, and he wanted to move away. Someone said merrily that a general should be able to stand fire, and Washington riposted, "But it doesn't look good if he receives it from behind."[19]

---

[19] Maybe I didn't tell it right.

John Adams

1797–1801

★

In the beginning there were Adamses all over the place, and nothing satisfied them. They expected a lot of themselves, and each other, and total strangers, and made life difficult for miles around.

It was never easy being an Adams, and marrying them was even worse. It was the kind of family where nobody ever said dumb things like "Hot enough for you?" or "Have a nice day" or "How about those Mets?" They only talked about lofty things like political economy and ethical principles and astronomy and international relations. In every generation a child cracked under the strain and took to drink or suicide, and the ones who survived scarcely knew a carefree moment.

All the Adams men were very bright and had no patience with people who weren't bright enough to see things their way. They even let their wives be bright, so at least one person would see things their way, but this wasn't always enough. The only wife to give full satisfaction was Abigail, and the other wives got pretty fed up with hearing about her.

Harry Truman said Abigail would have made a better president than John, but I don't know. She had a lot more charm and tact,[1] but she was a flaming radical and wanted to free the slaves, educate the children, declare war on France, and tax whiskey. She even mentioned votes for women. John said, "I cannot but laugh, you are so saucy."

John and Abigail met when she was a shy old maid of eighteen, and everyone says she was plain as a boot, but in her portraits she has the alert, considering look of a Jane Austen heroine and certainly didn't frighten the horses. He was no rosebud himself. He was conceited and high-minded and prickly and rude and penniless and short and given to fits of rage and depression, but she married him anyway. He was the only man who'd asked her.

---

[1] So does your average warthog.

They were married for fifty-four years and just adored each other.[2] Their "Dearest Friend" letters make some of history's happier reading, and when she died he told John Quincy that without her he "could not have endured, or even survived." He wrote, "Nothing has contributed so much to support my mind as the choice blessing of a wife whose capacity enabled her to understand, and whose pure virtue obliged her to approve, the views of her husband."

If all this sounds pretty pure and intellectual, it wasn't. She wrote saying the thought of him coming home made her shake all over. When she twitted him about being sixty, he wrote saying if he had her within grabbing distance he'd soon convince her he wasn't a minute past forty.

Maybe the Adamses were a nuisance to have around the house, but without them we'd be an extension of Greater Canada right this minute, and you'd be drinking milk in your tea and watching cricket matches that lasted for weeks on end.

John and Abigail and John's cousin Sam were about the only people who thought we should dump England completely. Everyone else figured we could work something out if we just sat down and talked it over like sensible adults, but the Adamses were dead set on divorce. They're the reason you think the whole Revolution happened in Boston.

John and Abigail lived in suburban Braintree[3] on a dear little farm. He chopped wood and practiced law and planted barley and talked politics. She cooked and sewed and had five children and talked politics. They were against the taxes, of course, and so are you, but you get them all muddled up. That's all right. Everyone does.

---

[2] They were separated a lot and that probably helped. Spending *every* day with John would try the patience of a spaniel. Go ask the Continental Congress.

[3] Presently it turned out to be called Quincy, after Abigail's grandfather.

To start with, England needed some money and thought we were as good a place as any to find it, so they sent us the Revenue, or Sugar, Act of 1764. This was a tax on foreign sugar and silk and linen and Madeira, the preferred tipple of the better sort of colonial. They followed this Act with the Stamp Act of 1765, which said that we had to pay anywhere from a halfpenny to twenty shillings sterling for stamps to paste on all our newspapers, broadsides, pamphlets, licenses, commercial bills, notes and bonds, advertisements, almanacs, leases, and any other flat surface they could think of.

This was a silly nuisance and made all the more important people hopping mad. John told everyone not to buy any stamps, and crowds of colonials followed the stamp officers around town calling them names, and burned them in effigy and set fire to their houses. In 1766 the English realized they couldn't get rich on stamps and repealed the idea, but the Revenue Act stayed, and on top of it they slapped a tax on paint, lead, paper, and tea. John said nobody should buy those things either, and people stopped painting their houses and switched from tea and Madeira to New England rum. It had a kick like an ostrich, and the Sons of Liberty joined hands and danced around and around the Liberty Tree, an elm conveniently close to Boston Common. Switching from tea to rum didn't exactly start the Revolution, but it didn't slow it down any either.

The main cause of the Revolution, aside from all those Adamses, was the quantity of feisty, short-tempered people on this side of the Atlantic at the time, and the quantity of unusually bossy, fatheaded chumps on the other side, topped by poor George III, who suffered from funny feelings in his head. After a while, though, even the English realized they were losing money because we weren't buying the nice things they sent us, so they repealed all the taxes except the one on tea.

They kept that just to show us who was boss.

It was only three cents on the pound, but it was the principle of the thing. They never asked us if we wanted to pay a sales tax. Now that we have our own government, they always ask us if we want to pay taxes, and we always say certainly, we'd be delighted. It makes all the difference.

The *Dartmouth,* the *Eleanor,* and the *Beaver* sailed into Boston Harbor full of tea, and the governor wouldn't let them leave again, so we threw the tea in the water and after that nobody wanted it.[4]

The history books want us to think the Boston Tea Party was the social event of the season,[5] but by contemporary accounts, it was pretty dull. Some 60 to 150 persons, depending on which book you believe, dressed up as Indians and went quietly on board, and nobody tried to stop them, and they opened the chests and deep-sixed them and went home to bed. Afterward "the stillest night succeeded, which Boston had enjoyed for several months."

Nobody ever found out who the Indians were. A lot of people claimed to know later, but the actual Indians never said a word. Probably the Adamses weren't there. At least, when John turned up the next morning, he said he'd been at Plymouth court on his circuit, and for all I know he was. Anyway, he was tickled pink.

The British weren't. When it came to private property they never could take a joke, and they closed Boston Harbor and sent troops and were mad as a wet hen. One chap in Parliament wanted everyone in Boston flogged and the town "knocked down about their ears and destroyed."

Well, you all remember how the war began, with the various dustups like Lexington and Concord, where Paul Revere got his famous horse captured by the British and had to walk home. Then in 1776 somebody noticed it was the

---

[4] Boston Harbor was cleaner then, but not *that* clean.
[5] "Howling," "riotous," "mob," and "unruly" are the usual words.

Fourth of July, so we said we were independent, but the British took no notice whatever. The *London Morning Post* gave it six lines on an inside page.

After many exciting battles we got up to 1783, and John Adams and Ben Franklin and John Jay cooked up the peace treaty in Paris. It gave us everything east of the Mississippi and in between Canada and Florida.[6] People call this the greatest diplomatic feat in the history of the United States, but all I can say is, it's a good thing Franklin was there or we'd still be sniping at redcoats. He was one smooth operator and romanced all the old ladies and everyone loved him. Adams barged around being rude and impatient, and nobody liked him nearly as much, or bought him an aperitif or said *bonjour,* and his feelings were hurt. The Adamses' feelings were always hurt when people didn't like them. They could never understand it.

What with the Continental Congresses, and being envoy to France and Holland and minister to Great Britain, years and years went by when John hardly set foot on the farm. Abigail milked the cows and studied Latin so she could teach little John Quincy, and reported on the political gossip in New England. They wrote each other bales of letters full of politics and manure and cows and useful advice, like painting a strip of tar around the apple trees to keep out the tent caterpillars.[7] He wrote that all time was wasted that was "not employed in farming, innocent, healthy, gay, elegant amusement!"[8]

---

[6] Spain got Florida, but who needed it? Disney World was still crawling with rattlesnakes and you couldn't get a hotel room south of St. Augustine.

[7] I've tried this. It fools some of the tent caterpillars some of the time.

[8] Washington and Jefferson were always saying the same thing. Farming looks like more fun from a safe distance.

By 1789, things had calmed down enough for us to have a proper government, and John went off to be Vice-President for eight years and President for four.

When he took office as President in 1797, he was greeted by widespread gloom. He wasn't all *that* popular—he'd squeaked in by three electoral votes—and everyone thought George Washington hung the moon and ought to stay forever. John moved into the presidential mansion all by himself, because Abigail was back home farming and being sick. There weren't any chairs or sheets or blankets because everything had belonged to George and Martha, and they'd taken it with them. Then Rhode Island sent him a cheese weighing 110 pounds and it just seemed like the last straw. Anyone would get discouraged, living in a house with a 110-pound cheese and no chairs, and besides, his teeth hurt. Abigail didn't show up to straighten things out until May, and in the meantime he just sat on the cheese and felt sorry for himself.

Thomas Jefferson was his Vice-President, due to the amusing notion of awarding this office to the first runner-up in the election.[9] Adams was a Federalist and Jefferson was a Republican, and by this time they had no use for each other. Jefferson said Adams was "distrustful, obstinate, excessively vain, and takes no counsel from anyone."[10] Jefferson, who had never met one, thought the common man had a kind of simple, natural nobility that would see us through. Adams thought the common man was just as selfish as the rest of us, and not half so well educated.

They didn't agree on anything, and neither did anyone else. Take France, for instance. By this time they'd had the

---

[9] After this misalliance they changed the rules, and the number-two candidate now gets to be Miss Congeniality instead, and weeps for joy.

[10] Especially from Jefferson.

French Revolution, followed by the Reign of Terror, Napoleonic Wars, and general Gallic confusion. Jefferson and half the country thought their Revolution was just as pure and high-minded as ours and we ought to rejoice in it. The Adamses and the other half complained that they'd killed off our old buddies there and besides, it was childish to go on and *on* roasting people alive and chopping their heads off like that.[11] Some hotheads like Abigail thought we should join England in fighting France, and Washington was hauled off his veranda to be commander in chief again, just in case.

Then there were the Alien and Sedition Acts, saying that if you were a dangerous-looking enemy alien the President could send you home and no one should print malicious lies against the government. Jefferson said this was tyranny, and people could print anything they pleased, and it just proved the states should run things for themselves.

It was pretty tense for a while, but then Adams arranged a sort of agreement with France and we didn't go to war after all. He said he wanted it as an epitaph: "Here lies John Adams, who took upon himself the responsibility of peace with France in the year 1800."

Folks thought this was a dreadful anticlimax, and muttered that if "the old woman" had been in town, we'd be over there fighting by now, all right, all right.

Abigail spent a lot of time back home in Quincy (or Braintree) to escape from the medical attentions of Dr. Benjamin Rush. She had diabetes, and rheumatism, and chronic remitting fever, and his bleedings and purges made her feel all wobbly. Dr. Rush was the most famous doctor in the country, but you couldn't convince him people didn't contain at least twenty-five pounds of blood and ought to get rid of most of it. Actually, we've only got a bit more than twelve

---

[11] They thought a few token roastings would have been plenty. Others thought you can never have too many.

pounds, and he was often disappointed when his patients ran dry, but it didn't stop him for a minute.[12]

Adams stayed in Philadelphia and had awful head colds and infected teeth and scaly eruptions on his hands and feelings of impending doom. (Washington had had smallpox, tuberculous pleurisy, malaria, bacillary dysentery, carbuncles, flu, typhoid, and pneumonia, though not all at once. Martha was always making everyone take pinkroot for the ague, but pinkroot doesn't help as much as you might think. Patrick Henry felt that lots and lots of opium was the only answer, and it did help, but most people just muddled along feeling rotten.)

The newspapers were never a bit nice to poor John, and called him things like "old, querulous, blind, crippled, toothless."[13] It's true he'd lost some of his hair, and his eyes bothered him, but he wasn't crippled and he certainly wasn't old, not compared to how old he got later. And they called him a spendthrift, which was silly—he only had two horses for his carriage, and Washington always had six and wanted more, but does the press notice details like that?

They got worse as the next election got closer. Back then, the actual candidates didn't campaign, which would have been undignified, but their supporters made up for it in spades and made allegations of a nonpolitical nature such as we'd blush to hear today, maybe. Jefferson's backers accused Adams of listening to his wife. They called him "His Rotundity" and "a mere old woman and unfit to be President." His own side retorted that Jefferson was going to write an atheist Bible and make everyone read it.

It took all winter to count the votes, and in the meantime

---

[12] Rush made a number of important scientific advances, such as discovering that the dark color of Negro skin is actually a disease, somewhat like leprosy.

[13] And Nixon thought they were kicking *him* around.

the Adamses had to pack up and move to Washington, which was supposed to be finished by then but wasn't. The whole area looked like a bomb site. Cities never get finished on time.

Everyone knows Abigail hung her laundry in the East Room in the White House to dry. They go on about it as if she spent her entire life hanging her laundry in the East Room, and frankly I'm sick of the whole subject. Look, there was no place else to put it, not even a fence outside to sling the sheets over. Nothing but mud and tree stumps and piles of construction trash. And wasn't it enough that she had to wash the stuff in the first place in water hand-hauled from half a mile away? And that the plaster was still wet and there was nobody to chop firewood and her rheumatism was killing her, and there weren't half enough candles, and no privy and the staircase wasn't finished, and workmen underfoot the whole time? Anyone else would have let the sheets stay dirty, and I don't want to hear another word about where she strung her clothesline.

By February everyone got sick of counting votes and decided Jefferson had won. Of all the early Presidents right up to Martin Van Buren, who was an airhead, only Adams and his son J.Q. got turned down for a second term. They were completely mystified by it.

So John was finally allowed to retire with his beloved wife to his beloved farm in Braintree (or Quincy), where he lived on for years and years and years and was bored sick.

Everyone seems to think it was almost miraculously strange that Adams and Jefferson died on the same day, July 4, 1826, the fiftieth anniversary of the Declaration of Independence. I don't know why they find this so amazing. We all have to go sometime.

Thomas Jefferson

1801–1809

★

Thomas Jefferson was an interesting and talented man and there are plenty of things you should want to know about him besides Sally Hemings. However, I suppose you won't be able to concentrate until you hear about Sally, so we might as well get it over with.

Many fairly responsible historians are now suggesting that Jefferson was having an affair with Sally. They keep calling her a teenage slave, even after this alleged thirty-eight-year affair, and agree that he was the father of her five children. Some agree that he was the father of her seven children, and some that he was the father of at least some of her numberless children.

Other historians shrug off the matter as too ridiculous to discuss.

All right, listen. When Jefferson was minister to France he sent for his younger daughter, Polly, who'd been living with relatives since her mother died. He wanted her fetched by some mature and responsible lady, but instead they sent Sally. Abigail Adams met them in London, and she thought Sally was unusually childish for fourteen and probably wouldn't be any use at all. Then she posted the girls on to Paris, and the first thing Jefferson did was buy both of them some new clothes. The clothes are exhibit A. It's the clothes that really get to people. Why, they ask, would he buy clothes for Sally unless there was something funny going on? Now, we are looking at a little slave girl from the backwoods of Virginia, and expecting the American minister to have her escorting his daughter in the Champs Elysées wearing a calico apron and a hanky on her head, for heaven's sake. And I suppose it doesn't make any difference that he was madly in love with Maria Cosway at the time.[1] Or that

---

[1] Maria had him in such a tizzy that he was walking along beside the Seine thinking about her and jumped over a fence and fell and dislocated his wrist. It hurt for months. He was no kid.

none of his worst enemies mentioned it until years later when he was President, and all of a sudden a fellow named Callender, who'd been turned down for a government job, wrote about it as if he'd been hiding under the bed.[2] And that nobody paid the slightest attention until quite recently, and now it's Sally, Sally, Sally everywhere you go.

What makes it so exciting is that she was a slave, and in those days there was a sharp distinction between black slave women and free white women, as the former could be beaten, raped, and sold by their owners, and the latter only by their male relatives, who always had their best interests at heart. The implication is that Sally couldn't have said no.[3] Everyone shivers with delicious horror at the thought that when Long Tom said "bedtime" she had to hop right in. Let's pull ourselves together—this is Thomas Jefferson, not Henry VIII. He had a pompous streak in him a yard wide, and when it came to ethics and the moral conduct of life he thought he was the greatest thing since the star of Bethlehem. He just could never have spoken to himself again if he'd carried on like that even once, let alone for thirty-eight years. And that's another thing. How many men do *you* know so stubborn they'd keep forcing the same unwilling woman into the sheets for thirty-eight years?

If she could have said no, then it's none of our business, but personally I don't believe a word of it. I'm sorry, because it would be nice to think he had someone to warm up his poor bony old feet, with Martha dying so young and all, but it didn't happen because it couldn't have. Not Tom. And I don't care if Sally had forty children. Tom wasn't the only

---

[2] Disappointed office seekers were an occupational hazard. Jefferson got off easy compared to poor Garfield.

[3] If she'd wanted to, that is. He was a bit of a catch, if you don't mind tall, handsome, famous, red-haired geniuses who play the violin.

man on the mountain, you know. Now, please try to stop thinking about it.

Jefferson's mother was a Randolph. This may not make any difference to you, but in Virginia it made a difference. However, Tom didn't like her very much and never mentioned her in public. Probably he found her intellectually inferior. She had ten children.

As a teenager he was one of those self-righteous types full of maxims about hard work, and when he fell in love with Rebecca Burwell, he brooded that it might interfere with his studies. Later he put her out of his mind and practiced law and managed his lands and went to the Virginia House of Burgesses.

For a fellow who considered himself a simple farmer,[4] he spent a lot of time politicking. After the Burgesses he was a delegate to the First Continental Congress, governor of Virginia, commercial envoy to France in charge of whale oil, salted fish, etc., and then succeeded Franklin as minister to France, where he tried to do something about the Barbary pirates, but nothing can be done about Barbary pirates. He was Washington's Secretary of State, Adams's Vice-President, and President. And whenever he got a chance, he went back home to Monticello and tore it down and started building it again differently. He spent most of his life building and unbuilding Monticello. It was a great nuisance for his wife.

He married Martha Wayles in 1772. I don't have any pictures of her, but family tradition says she was beautiful and musically talented.[5] He seems to have burned all their letters, so I don't have any gossip on their courtship, except that his idea of showing a girl a good time was to take his violin over to her house and play it all evening. No one will tell me whether he was any good on the thing, and few

---

[4] Or, alternately, a simple scientist and a simple architect.
[5] That is what families are here for.

sounds are more painful than those made by a person who's only fair to middling on the violin, but anyway she married him. In the ten years before she died, she had six children. Two of them, or about par for the course, lived to grow up.

Jefferson was a dreadful father, always writing to his motherless little girls that if they expected him to like them, they'd better study harder. He wrote the younger one telling her never to go out in the sun without a bonnet "because it will make you very ugly and then we should not love you so much."[6] Martha, Jr. (called Patsy) kept trying to please him, but Mary (called Polly or Maria) hardly knew him and didn't care, and small wonder.

His grandchildren remembered him fondly. Apparently he lightened up later.

He wrote the Declaration of Independence, or at least the first draft. Adams and Franklin made some changes, and then the congressional committee made some more. Everyone's an editor. (See Appendix II.) Congress didn't get around to signing it until August, but on July 4 they said they liked it just fine and wouldn't make any more changes, so there's no reason not to go on having our Fourth of July picnics on the Fourth of July.

Jefferson was a man of many interests. When he was in France and supposed to be looking after American matters there, he was often found traveling around studying other people's gardens and architecture and writing down what he thought of them. He wrote a large book called *Notes on the State of Virginia,* in which he explained all sorts of things, some of them concerning Virginia.

He liked his comforts. When he went to Philadelphia to be Secretary of State, he had to spend months rebuilding the house he planned to rent for a couple of years, so he could arrange all his things properly. He had 104 crates of stuff

---

[6] The "we" was editorial, or Queen Victorian.

shipped from France, including 38 chairs, 6 stoves, a waffle iron, 22 bellpulls, and 145 rolls of wallpaper, plus a lot of books. He liked to spend his afternoons buying books.[7]

Having all that stuff to pack up again would make some people think twice about moving, but three years later he'd had enough of being Secretary of State and went back to Monticello, where he found the fields in terrible shape. He rode around doing all the right things, like rotating crops and planting clover to improve the soil, but nobody could improve the soil at Monticello. It was on top of a mountain, because Tom liked the view. There is no good dirt on top of mountains. This has to do with the Law of Gravity.

He planted nine hundred peach trees and opened a small nail-making shop, and spent many happy hours counting and measuring nails. By 1796 he was turning out a ton of nails a month, but nobody wanted to buy them and they kept piling up. Then he won a medal for improving the moldboard plow. In his spare time he pulled down some more of Monticello and added a dome, and made plans to take off the roof.

But Tom was an Aries and easily bored, and pretty soon he was back in politics again, and before you knew it he was President.[8]

To show he was just a simple farmer, he slopped around the White House in "an old brown coat, red waistcoat, old corduroy smallclothes, much soiled—woolen hose—and slippers without heels." Some visitors were offended, but he did change for dinner, which was just as well since he went riding every afternoon and smelled of horse.

Three times a week he gave intimate little dinner parties

---

[7] Adams said Jefferson was indolent, but he wasn't. He was always busy doing something or other.

[8] In his inaugural address he said various things about entangling alliances and so on, but nobody heard a word. His voice was described as "almost femininely soft and gentle."

for twelve, and everyone sat at a round table so that nobody would seem more important than anyone else. People who really were more important than anyone else were furious, and the British ambassador and his wife were so mad they moved to Philadelphia.[9] At dinner, topics of an enlightening nature were discussed, and Jefferson showed off scientific curiosities like his revolving shelves for sneaking food into the room, and a waterproof raincoat from England, and the first Baked Alaska, containing America's first ice cream.

A church in Massachusetts sent him a twelve-hundred-pound cheese, and two years later he was still trying to make people eat some of it for dessert. It wasn't very good, but it certainly was big. Even bigger than Adams's.

Jefferson always wrote his own letters and speeches, so his secretary, Meriwether Lewis, didn't have anything to do but sharpen the pens and clean his fingernails with the penknife. Then Tom hit on the idea of sending him and William Clark out to walk over to the Pacific Ocean and look around. He was interested in buying a lot of the real estate out there, and in case he did he wanted to know what he was getting.

When Lewis and Clark were well on their way he had Robert Livingston and James Monroe negotiate to buy the whole Louisiana Territory from Napoleon for $15 million, or three cents an acre. It was a good deal, besides settling the problem of having either France or Spain making faces at us across the Mississippi.

Lewis and Clark wrote back to say there was a whole lot of country out there, with assorted Indians in it.[10] They sent along a black-billed magpie and a prairie dog, which Jefferson

---

[9] Once he invited his butcher to dinner. I don't know whether this was a joke or not. Probably not.

[10] The Indians were still friendly. They hadn't figured out what we were up to yet.

forwarded to Charles Willson Peale in Philadelphia. Jefferson didn't need a magpie, as he already had a mockingbird he'd taught to peck seed from his lips and hop up the stairs after him. (He was the first President to be followed upstairs by a mockingbird.) Lewis and Clark also sent a quantity of large bones, some of them prehistoric and some of them just plain bones. Jefferson loved them all and spread them out on the floor and spent hours arranging them.

Since you'd be crazy to spend the summer in Washington before air-conditioning, he always went back to Monticello for a breath of air and a spot of building. When he had to return to his duties with his building lust unslaked, he revised the White House, and added two wings for useful purposes like stables, an ice house, and wine storage. He decided that the roof leaked and replaced it, though it was practically brand-new. He put a cistern in the attic, so water could dribble down through some pipes. He fixed up his clothes on a turnstile device, so his pants and jackets revolved, and built a fieldstone wall with an arch over the north entrance.

The truth was, he was getting bored again. He was a great man, but he had the attention span of a gnat.

Everyone begged him to stay for a third term, but he said no. His excuse was that there was nothing in the Constitution to keep a President from staying *forever* once he got his hooks into the thing, and he didn't want to set a bad example.

After this, he lost interest completely and got started with his packing. He had a lot to pack, and when people came to him asking what to do about his embargo on trade with Great Britain, and whether to leave it, or lift it, or strengthen it, or declare war, he said that was for the next man to figure out and went on with his packing. He said, "Never did a prisoner, released from his chains, feel such relief as I shall on shaking off the shackles of power."

When he got back home to Monticello, his daughter Martha and six of her eight children moved in with him, and it was all very jolly. He was so pleased that he built another house ninety miles away, called Poplar House, that was all octagons. He'd always been fond of a nice octagon. Even the privies were octagonal.[11]

Then he got started on the University of Virginia. It was a whole new building plan, arranged around pavilions, and he figured it would make Harvard and Yale look pretty sick.

It's not true that Jefferson introduced the tomato to America, or publicly ate one to prove they were edible. For one thing, the tomato was a native here to start with, and for another, lots of people had been eating them right along. It was just that people one knew didn't eat them, any more than they ate snails in garlic butter. When Jefferson was President he always noted down their first appearance in the Washington markets, and in 1809 they were on his own planting list, but he never ate one on the courthouse steps. There's a lot of nonsense talked about tomatoes, and you want to ignore most of it.

If you care, and some people hardly care at all, he did introduce Brussels sprouts to the United States in 1810.

He owed everyone money. His naillery wasn't any more successful than it ever was, and his crops were full of Hessian flies, whatever they are. He invested ten thousand dollars building a commercial gristmill, but somehow that didn't pan out either. Then he bought a spinning jenny and a loom, but it took two thousand yards a year just to make clothes for his family and slaves, and there wasn't much left to sell.

After the British burned the Library of Congress in 1814 he sold the country his books for $23,950. This left him with plenty of debts still unpaid and nothing to read. He was

---

[11] He was broke and in debt, but he couldn't stop himself.

trying to organize a lottery to sell Monticello and raise some money when he died.

He wrote his own epitaph, which is the only way to do it if you want it done right. It says, "Here was Buried Thomas Jefferson, Author of the Declaration of Independence, of the Statute of Virginia for Religious Freedom and Father of the University of Virginia."

Finicky people think Jefferson was a terrible President because he believed in states' rights and a weak central government. On the other hand, he was the only President to invent the pedometer, the dumbwaiter, the lazy Susan, and the swivel chair. Try to imagine America without swivel chairs.[12]

Jefferson didn't free his slaves when he died. He'd always thought that slavery was a revolting, abominable custom, and that one of these days somebody would abolish it, but in the meantime there it was and what can you do?

---

[12] Or Brussels sprouts.

James Madison

1809–1817

★

ittle Jemmy Madison was not an inconsiderable person. He'd been an important fellow at the Constitutional Convention, and was called the Father of the Constitution.[1] He was coauthor of the *Federalist Papers,* everyone's bedside favorite, and Jefferson's Secretary of State and personal choice for President.

Just the same, he *looked* like an inconsiderable person. He was only five foot four and didn't weigh a hundred pounds with rocks in his hat, and if it hadn't been for his wife Dolley people would scarcely have noticed him, and would have walked smack into him in the halls, and forgotten to pass him the potatoes.[2]

Dolley Madison grew up all dressed in gray in a strict Quaker family, and her father made and sold laundry starch in the parlor. When even this modest enterprise collapsed, he locked himself in his bedroom for the rest of his life. He felt he was a failure.[3] So Dolley married a Mr. Todd, who died, and then Aaron Burr introduced her to Madison.

Jemmy had never thought much about women, but he was forty-three and felt it was time to get married, and he might as well marry Dolley, who was only twenty-five and had dimples. Dolley wasn't sure. It took her all summer to decide, and then when she did write to say yes it took Jemmy three days to answer her letter.

So they got married, and fell in love and lived happily ever after. She called him "my darling little husband."[4] He said that whenever his official duties gave him a headache, he went and found Dolley and had a chat and felt 100 percent better. She was that kind of girl.

---

[1] Not often, though. As a nickname, it lacks clout.
[2] You yourself would think of him only when counting your five-thousand-dollar bills.
[3] He was.
[4] She could have broken him over her knee like a stick of kindling, but she didn't want to.

Dolley didn't care a fig for politics, just for chatting and visiting and giving perfectly marvelous parties and making sure everyone was happy. She'd been Jefferson's hostess when he was President, so that gave her sixteen years as queen of Washington, and she loved every minute of it and so did Washington. In that whole piranha tank she didn't have a single enemy, except some sourpusses who hadn't been invited.[5] Even John Adams liked her.

Her portraits are kind of disappointing—she didn't like them either—but in person she bowled everyone over and they fought to get into what Washington Irving called "the blazing splendor" of her drawing room. All the women wore what Dolley wore. When Dolley took snuff, everyone thought it was charming and took snuff too. When Dolley bought a pet macaw, everyone else bought a pet macaw and the jungles of South America fell silent. No murmur of scandal about her ever got murmured. She was the kindest, merriest, most generous woman in town, with an endless appetite for fun, and made everyone learn to waltz.

Out in the world, Jefferson had left us in kind of a mess with the Brits again, and they wouldn't give up their unfortunate habit of dragging our seamen off to work on their ships instead of ours. Some people even thought they were egging the Shawnees on to do unpleasant things to our soldiers.[6] Other people said the whole thing was an excuse to take over Canada. Anyway, it turned into the War of 1812, known to his enemies as Madison's War.

It was a sloppy sort of war, and dragged on. Madison wanted to fortify the capital, but his Secretary of War said

---

[5] And a local preacher, who kept thundering that if she didn't quit giving parties on Sunday God was going to burn the White House down.

[6] Maybe and maybe not. The Shawnees were pretty blistered without any egging.

nonsense, the British were after Baltimore, not Washington.[7] He was wrong.[8] By August of 1814 you could hear the war quite clearly from the East Room. Jemmy rushed off to Bladensburg to take command of an artillery battery, but when he noticed how dangerous this was he got back in his carriage and drove away. He'd never said he was a hero.

Back home, Dolley was planning the usual party, but she was having trouble getting guests. A Mrs. E. Jones sent regrets for the evening's dinner, explaining that her husband was busy dispatching Marines to defend the city.[9] She added, "There appears to be rather serious cause for apprehension."

Jemmy had left a hundred men to guard the White House, but they didn't last long. The kindlier historians suggest that they all rushed away to enlist, but wherever they went, Dolley was left alone with a few servants and the steward. She postponed the party and packed up a few things—the national seal, the Declaration of Independence, the first draft of the Constitution, and a change of underwear. On second thought she added some forks and spoons and the yellow velvet curtains, and sent her macaw off to safety with the steward. Then she sat down to write a letter to her sister.

The next day she was still there, hoping Jemmy would be home in time for dinner. She got up on the roof to look for him, but all she could see were our gallant soldiers running as fast as they could. She went on with her dinner plans, of course, and the letter to her sister. She wrote, "Here I am, within sound of the cannon. Mr. Madison comes not. . . . Two messengers, covered with dust, come to bid me fly; but here I mean to wait for him."

---

[7] He didn't explain why.
[8] He got fired for it, too, and replaced by James Monroe—up next.
[9] They didn't.

Finally a friend, Charles Carroll, came to drag her out bodily, but she insisted on rescuing the Stuart-Winstanley portrait of Washington. It turned out to be screwed solidly into the wall, so she had the frame smashed, and rolled up the canvas and handed it out the door to what she described as two gentlemen from New York who were passing by.[10] Then she finished her letter: "And now, dear sister, I must leave this house, or the retreating Army will make me a prisoner in it by filling up the road. . . . When I shall again write to you, or where I shall be tomorrow, I cannot tell!"

She seems to have had the time of her life. She never suggested for a minute that Jemmy might have stuck around to take care of her and the White House instead of making an ass of himself playing war. She never mentioned that she was being rather stalwart to hold the fort and rescue some vital items of government, not to mention the velvet curtains. She was just planning a party, and waiting for Jemmy, and then she had to leave to beat the rush hour and, of course, the British, who dropped by several hours later[11] and burned the building down.[12]

They burned everything that looked official. Then it rained, and the whole city smoldered and smelled simply disgusting.

Philadelphia invited Madison to move the government back up there, and he did think about it, but Dolley was outraged. The Founding Fathers had said Washington, and Washington it was going to be.[13]

---

[10] They did too bring it back. It's still not exactly Van Gogh's *Sunflowers*, but it's in the White House, which is more than you can say for the rest of the furniture.

[11] They found the dinner table set for forty.

[12] Moral: Don't give parties on Sunday.

[13] You couldn't get people to come to parties in Philadelphia. You still can't.

They moved into a nice unburned house on Lafayette Square, and Dolley gave bigger and bigger parties until people complained of the crush, but they kept on coming just the same.

Cheered and cosseted by his wife, little Jemmy lived to be eighty-five, and after he died Dolley was still Dolley. She moved back to Washington from his place in Virginia and gave people advice about their parties. She grew to be a merry old lady, and found the perfect girl for Martin Van Buren's son to marry, and helped John Tyler with his social life, and played whist with John Quincy Adams, and even managed to befriend the unfriendly Polks.

She never had been a beauty, but some people thought she was because she made them feel so good. Even the British ambassador, meeting her for the first time, said our plump Dolley looked "every inch a queen."

Several Presidents' wives were hardly any use at all, but Jemmy did okay.

James Monroe

1817–1825

★

James Monroe is remembered for the Monroe Doctrine, which some consider John Quincy Adams's finest achievement. John Quincy was Secretary of State, and he was sick and tired of France and Spain and England sniffing around our continents, and Russians sneaking their trading posts down from Alaska as far as San Francisco.[1] His Monroe Doctrine says that since Europeans are basically different from Americans, from now on nobody but us could bully the new South American republics or set up colonies in our hemisphere or bother our neighbors, and in return we wouldn't meddle in European affairs either.[2]

Nobody in Europe or South America paid the slightest attention to the thing, and Monroe didn't care much either. He was interested in Greece. Greece was fighting for independence from the Turks, and Monroe wanted us to go help. People got all worked up about Greece, and made their sons learn Greek in school and ran around building Greek Revival courthouses and pretending they'd read Thucydides. Daniel Webster said the Greeks were a lot more fun than the "inhabitants of the Andes and the dwellers on the borders of the Vermilion Sea."[3]

John Quincy was always knocking himself out on projects that nobody else cared about.[4]

Be honest, now. Tell me three things you know about Guyana. Tell me one. Find Paraguay on a map. Find South America on a map. Well, as far as I know Monroe couldn't either. He had his own troubles, same as you and I.

---

[1] He made them back off all the way to 54°40′ where they belonged.
[2] So we changed our mind. Big deal.
[3] There is no Vermilion Sea. Daniel Webster was a great orator, and that's the way great orators talk.
[4] He bought Florida from Spain and nobody cared about that either.

James Monroe was a Virginian and went to William and Mary, but he dropped out to fight in the Revolution and get wounded at the Battle of Trenton. He was aide to General Stirling, a famous alcoholic, and between them they emptied many a glass. After this early training James was known as a deep, even an enthusiastic, drinker, but no one suggested he went reeling around the White House singing improper songs. He was always a gentleman. He even looked like a gentleman, in an eighteenth-century sort of way, and kept on wearing knee breeches and buckled shoes for ages after everyone else gave theirs to the Goodwill. He had a dimple in his chin and nice, kind blue-gray eyes and was said to resemble George Washington,[5] though I can't see it myself.

He wasn't terribly clever—John Adams called him "dull, heavy, and stupid"—but he was honest and amiable and people liked him.[6] He studied law under Jefferson, and Madison made him Secretary of State and War, both at once. His wife was a famous beauty who turned out to be a mistake.

People said Elizabeth Monroe looked regal, and it's true there's a suggestion of the Tudors about her portrait, but that might be the ermine. Dolley Madison's dear friend Mrs. Seaton said Mrs. Monroe "paints very much and has, besides, an appearance of youth which would induce a stranger to suppose her age to be thirty." Actually Elizabeth's daughter Eliza would never see thirty again; nineteenth-century cosmetics can't have been as primitive as you'd think.

There was a younger daughter, Maria, born when Eliza was already seventeen, and only one child that died in between. I realize it's none of my business, but this wasn't a terribly generous output for a lady of the times, and from what we hear of Mrs. M. she may have been a martyr to bedtime headaches. James deserved better.

---

[5] This was considered a compliment.
[6] Except John Adams, but there's no pleasing an Adams.

Washington found her an awful letdown after dear Dolley. She thought the whole town was beneath her notice socially, and refused to see visitors. Dolley used to hand out punch and seedcake to everyone who dropped in, even if she didn't know their names, but Mrs. Monroe thought they should wait for formal invitations, and then she didn't send any. She didn't make calls, either. Eliza and her husband moved into the White House, and when somebody had to be visited, Eliza went instead. Mrs. M. said she had a headache.

The French minister gave a grand ball to celebrate foreign troops pulling out of France, and the Monroes wouldn't go. Mrs. Monroe said Eliza could go, but only if nobody mentioned it or told the reporters. The French minister was furious.

When little Maria got married in the East Room, no one was invited. The Russian minister asked what gift he could send, and Eliza told him to skip it. The Russian minister was furious.

Everyone was furious, and kept hanging around John Quincy's office complaining so he couldn't get any work done.[7] He was too busy to make calls himself and grumbled about "this senseless war of etiquette visiting."[8]

Pretty soon women stopped going to the White House even when they did get invited. When Mrs. Monroe gave her Tuesday night receptions nobody showed up but her sisters, and there wasn't a sound except the teacups clinking in their saucers.

In spite of his womenfolk everyone voted to reelect Monroe, and his administration was called The Era of Good

---

[7] Amaze your friends: Monroe's Vice-President was named D. D. Tompkins. Apparently he wasn't much help.

[8] Washington wasn't exactly London. If you didn't visit, you could stand around throwing sticks into the Potomac, or you could take a nap.

Feeling because there was only one political party and it was hard to scrape up much of a fight.

Of course, there was the matter of the furniture. It was kind of a furniture administration right from the start.

After Monroe was elected the first time, the White House was supposed to be all rebuilt and ready by the following fall, but you know contractors, and even when the roof was finished there still wasn't anything to sit on. It was nice to have that George Washington portrait Dolley rescued, but it wasn't very practical. You can't sit on a portrait, or at least not on a portrait of Washington. So Monroe sold the government his own furniture for $9,071.22½, which fixed up two bedrooms and the state dining room. It was mostly Louis Seize stuff, and mighty elegant. Mrs. Monroe had expensive tastes. Then a Colonel Lane got some money and scurried around filling in the gaps.[9] The Monroes ordered all the important pieces from France, and the French charged them prices they felt would do honor to the "President's palace."

Congress nearly choked when they saw the bills, and then, toward the end of the second term, they added them up and noticed there was twenty thousand dollars missing. Congressman Cocke asked Monroe to stop by and explain this to a congressional committee, and Monroe sent a message back saying to "tell Cocke he was a scoundrel." Then he grandly offered to buy back his own things for the original $9,071.22½. This didn't quite clear the matter up, and it got kind of sordid. Nobody ever did find the twenty thousand dollars, but I'm sure Colonel Lane would have had some perfectly simple explanation if he hadn't been dead already.[10]

---

[9] He paid $9.56¼ for a mustard pot, but I'm sure it was a lovely one.

[10] Nobody asked Mrs. Monroe about it. They were scared of her.

After they left the White House, Mrs. Monroe kept right on buying expensive decorative accessories, and James got poorer and poorer until he was quite surrounded by Louis Seize candelabra and stony-broke.

He died on the Fourth of July, like Adams and Jefferson, but by this time people had come to expect it.

A biographer said, "His virtue was not in flying high but in walking orderly, his talents were exercised not in grandeur but in mediocrity." So what's this biographer fellow done that's so special, I'd like to know?

John Quincy Adams

1825–1829

★

John Adams had always felt that the presidency should be, well, not *hereditary,* which would be undemocratic, but just naturally reserved for a group of the right sort of families whose sons would be properly educated and trained for public service, and they'd just naturally run things because they'd know what was best for the rest of us rabble.

Small wonder people were suspicious when his son showed up.

John Quincy was an Adams through and through. His wife Louisa said sadly, "As regards women, the Adams family are one and all peculiarly harsh and severe in their characters. There seems to exist no sympathy, no tenderness for the weakness of the sex."[1] She was a pretty girl and a scholar, and read Greek and wrote French poetry and played the harp, but who was good enough for the Adamses? She was said to suffer from melancholia, and no wonder. There were Adamses everywhere she turned. She saw Adamses in her sleep. Even her children were Adamses.

John Quincy had always worked hard to be a credit to the family, and his father was very supportive and wrote things like "If you do not rise to the head not only of your profession but of your country, it will be owing to your own *laziness, slovenliness,* and *obstinacy.*" As for his mother, his grandson Brooks says J.Q. loved her best of anyone in the world. I suppose he and Abigail were always going off into the kitchen for a heart-to-heart about political economy and leaving Louisa alone, muttering Greek choruses to herself.

He even looked a little like Abigail, at least for a while. In the Copley portrait he was twenty-eight and looks downright elfin, for an Adams. He looks like a poet, and in 1832 he did produce a slim volume, and maybe it's not Keats and

---

[1] She stuck it out for fifty years, though. He must have had *something.*

Shelley but it's still the only book of poems by an American President.[2]

Later he stopped looking like his mother and lost his hair and grew a tummy and looked like his father.

Way down inside he may have been a sensitive poet, but outside he was a toad, and even the nicer class of toad refused to have much to do with him, and warned their toad children against growing up like John Quincy. He even noticed it himself. He said, "I am a man of reserved, cold, austere, and forbidding manners. My political adversaries say a gloomy misanthrope; my personal enemies an unsocial savage."

He wore any old thing that came to hand. He wore the same hat for ten years. He got dreadful colds like his father and was always coughing and sniffling.[3] Lyttelton called him "doggedly and systematically repulsive. With a vinegar aspect, cotton in his leathern ears and hatred in his heart, he sat . . . like a bulldog among spaniels."

Kinder folk called him "an intellectual's intellectual," meaning there were only about five people in the country who understood a word he said. He and his father and Jefferson were our smartest Presidents, and John Quincy was probably the sanest of the three, but being smart and sane isn't everything. If you're an Adams, it can be downright irritating, and it was. When he'd run against Monroe in 1820 most people ignored him completely.[4] He didn't even win his own election, when you get right down to it.

There were four candidates, John Quincy, Andrew Jackson, Henry Clay, and a Mr. Crawford, and they were all

---

[2] Are you glad or sorry?

[3] Jefferson always soaked his feet in ice water every day to keep from catching colds, but as far as I know the Adamses never took this simple precaution.

[4] The electoral count was 231 to 1.

Republicans.[5] Jackson got 43 percent of the popular vote, and John Quincy got 30 percent, but neither had an electoral majority, so it went to the House. They argued about it till February, and agreed that John Calhoun was the Vice-President, but nobody was President. Finally Clay, who was Speaker, said Jackson wiping out twenty-five hundred Englishmen at the Battle of New Orleans wasn't quite the right resume, and swung the election to J.Q.[6]

Well, the Jacksonians howled bloody murder, but they might have gotten over it except for what Adams did next. Would you believe he made Clay Secretary of State? Of course the whole town thought there'd been some kind of deal, and Clay had to fight a duel with a hot-headed senator named Randolph about it, though they missed each other by a mile. The Jacksonians were beside themselves with rage and started plotting the next election right away, and vowed they'd never pass a bill Adams wanted, or replace the chairs and tables the Monroes took with them, or say hello to him on Pennsylvania Avenue. So much for the Era of Good Feeling.[7]

It was all a misunderstanding, as Adamses are above making deals, but it made an awful mess. However, try telling an Adams he's about to barge into a giant public-relations error. It just puts his back up. Adamses are above public relations too.[8]

John Quincy felt even worse about the election than Jackson did. He thought he deserved to win it fair and square,

---

[5] You can forget about the Federalists now, if you haven't already.

[6] Clay ran for President oftener than anyone, or anyone *mainstream,* and finally gave up and said he'd rather be right instead. It was just as well.

[7] Presently the Jacksonians decided to be Democrats, and the two-party system was back in business.

[8] This is their main problem.

since he'd worked hard for the country all his life, and been minister to everywhere, and a senator, and dreamed up the Monroe Doctrine while he was Secretary of State, and his father had always told him to be President, and now look. He thought seriously about turning it down, but not *that* seriously.

What he planned to do as President was jack up the general state of culture around here. He thought there should be a famous international university in Washington, with scholars and scientists clustering from all over the world like Athens or Charlemagne or something. The Jacksonians thought this was great nonsense, as they were all *non campus mentis,* or not university material. Most of all J.Q. wanted a national observatory, because there wasn't a single observatory in the whole country, and he thought if we had one in Washington we could look at the stars and that would make everything a lot nicer.[9] He called it a "lighthouse of the skies," and this struck Congress as a real thigh-slapper. They just howled. For months people stopped each other in the streets and said "lighthouse of the skies," and laughed till the tears ran down their cheeks.

He also thought we should build roads and canals so people could send things from place to place and there wouldn't be any more wars.[10] Nothing came of that either. The main piece of legislation that went through was the Tariff of Abominations, and it made the Southerners mad as hornets.

Congress wouldn't finish building the White House or buy any furniture, but they did grade and fill the outdoors, finally,

---

[9] Much later there was one in Cincinnati, and he almost killed himself traveling out there to dedicate it, but face it, Cincinnati isn't Washington.

[10] I forget how he'd worked that out, but it seemed to make sense at the time.

and John Quincy went out and puttered in it. He planted gardens, shrubs, orchards, strange vegetables nobody would eat, and a whole forest of tree seedlings. It made him feel a little better. He planted white mulberries for a silkworm plantation, and Louisa sat around soaking sticky little silkworm cocoons in warm water and unwinding the threads. It gave her something to do in the evenings. John Quincy liked to read some Cicero or Milton or Plutarch and go to bed early.

He always got up before dawn and walked four or five miles and then took off his clothes and went for a swim in the Potomac.[11] One morning a lady reporter he'd been dodging saw his bald head bobbling around in the river and sat down on his clothes and refused to budge till he gave her the interview. (This story turns up so often I suppose there might be something in it, unlikely as it seems. They say her name was Anne Royall.)

If J.Q. felt bad about the election of '24, he felt a lot worse about '28. It wasn't just losing, it was Andrew Jackson. He thought Jackson was the spirit of absolute evil, and his election proved once and for all that there was no God, and that meant he, J.Q., would never go to heaven and see his mother again.

Jackson's election proved nothing of the sort, of course, and just because he couldn't spell and liked to play with guns didn't prove he was the Antichrist, but you couldn't persuade J.Q.

He felt he was a total failure in life, because he'd always meant to "banish war and slavery from the face of the earth forever."[12] To top it off his oldest son, George Washington Adams, started seeing things that weren't there and killed himself.

---

[11] This was all very healthy, but it never did a *thing* for his figure.

[12] Did I mention that Adamses expect a lot of themselves?

John Quincy always expected the worst, and why not?

Then, just as life seemed darkest, some kindly people came and said he could be their congressman if he wanted. The other Adamses thought it was pretty low-rent for an ex-President to go back to Washington as a humble Congressman, but J.Q. said it wasn't, either, and back he went. He spent the next seventeen years there, still trying to wipe out the world's two oldest institutions with his bare hands and pretending not to mind what Jackson had done to his gardens. Sometimes he even thought he'd be invited to be President again. He never could understand why he was so unpopular, or what that had to do with being President anyway.

He even died in Congress, an Adams to the end. (See POLK.)

There were plenty of Adamses left, though. His son Charles Francis had a shot at being Vice-President in 1848, but his ticket lost to Taylor, who was a war hero. Adamses are never war heroes. Adamses *hate* wars. After that the family tended to lurk on the sidelines complaining about the low quality of Presidents nowadays, and writing books with depressing titles like *The Degradation of the Democratic Dogma,* which made surprisingly little difference to the electorate.

Many Americans rarely think about the Adamses, sometimes ignoring them for weeks on end. We seem to feel it wasn't quite necessary to have *two* short, bald, portly, intellectual Presidents with bad manners named John Adams.

Count your blessings. Considering the Adamses, if it weren't for Democracy and the American public, we could have had six or seven.

Andrew Jackson

1829–1837

★

Many of the wisest men in the country considered Jackson to be some kind of nut,[1] but they never could see a joke. He was just easily excited. At six foot one he weighed only 140 pounds, and had gray hair like a pigeon's nest and blue eyes with a rather unsettling glitter in them. He was Scots-Irish and never stopped to count to ten, and whenever he got his Irish up he challenged someone to a duel. Some say he fought in over a hundred, mostly because he thought people were talking about his wife.[2]

There was nothing wrong with his wife. Her name was Rachel, and it's true she smoked a pipe, but he was very attached to her just the same. Way back in 1790, Jackson was boarding in the same house with her and her husband, a Captain Lewis Robards, and Robards started complaining in the local pubs that he thought Andrew and Rachel were holding hands behind his back. When Jackson heard about this, he told Robards that if he ever said it again, "he would cut the ears out of his head, and that he was tempted to do it anyhow." Jackson was a man of his word in such matters, and he took to fingering a butcher's knife whenever Robards came into the room. Pretty soon Robards left town, glancing anxiously over his shoulder.

Jackson and Rachel found they had a lot in common, and later when they heard on the grapevine that Robards had gotten a divorce in Virginia they got married.[3]

Two years later it turned out that Robards hadn't quite gotten this divorce after all, so when it finally did come through they had to go get married all over again. It was embarrassing, but it could happen to anybody.

---

[1] "Ignorant, passionate and imbecile" and "fierce ungovernable temper" were some of the kindlier remarks. Jefferson said he couldn't possibly think of anyone worse to be President.

[2] He was so full of bullets he rattled like a bag of marbles.

[3] At least they said they did, and I believe it, even if nobody ever could find the records.

Jackson was touchy about it and kept his powder dry. When a man named Dickinson made some catty remark, he challenged him to a duel, though Dickinson could drill a dime at fifty yards and Jackson had terrible eyes and could hardly *see* a dime. He let Dickinson shoot first, and the bullet broke one of Jackson's ribs, and then he took extra-careful aim and shot Dickinson dead. He said, "I intended to kill him. I would have stood up long enough to kill him if he had put a bullet in my brain."

The whole story was nearly forty years old when he was running for President against John Quincy in 1828, but don't you know people went and dug it up? The *Cincinnati Gazette* rolled its eyes piously and said, "Ought a convicted adulteress and her paramour be placed in the highest office of this free and Christian land?" People went on and on about it, and when they got tired of abusing Rachel they said Jackson's mother was "a common prostitute brought to this country by British soldiers." It's a wonder anyone bothered, since a child could have seen Jackson was going to win.[4] But Rachel was sick as mud about it all, and it made her so nervous and depressed that shortly before he took office, she died.

Naturally Jackson blamed John Quincy Adams for it, but it wasn't Adams who started the talk, any more than it was Jackson who told everyone that Adams lurked around Catholic churches chatting in Latin with nuns and priests. In those primitive days, the candidates didn't have to come out and tell horrible lies about each other in person. Their fans and favorite newspapers did it for them and really put their backs into it.

The inauguration was the party of the year. Jackson was Old Hickory, hero of the Battle of New Orleans, and stood for all the manly American virtues like cockfighting, horse racing, drinking, gambling, and shooting at people. He was

---

[4] "Lighthouse of the skies," for heaven's sake.

the candidate of just plain folks, and they'd all[5] voted for him
and came to town to see him sworn in. The men had hickory-
wood stirrups and their wives wore strings of hickory nuts
around their necks. They camped out all over the place and
threw chicken bones around and galloped up and down firing
guns. Some fastidious observers said it put them in mind of
the barbarian hordes at the gates of Rome, while others
thought it was more like the French Revolution and the
peasants mincing up the aristocracy.

After the ceremony, everyone followed Jackson home and
crashed the White House party. They nearly killed him
fighting to shake hands, and they squeezed in through the
windows and climbed on the chairs with their boots on, and
women fainted and got trampled, and thousands of dollars
worth of glass and china got smashed, and bric-a-brac was
swiped for souvenirs, and the carpets and upholstery got all
squashy with mud and tobacco juice.[6] Finally enough of
them were lured outside with washtubs full of punch so
Jackson could escape to a hotel.

He couldn't complain, of course, because he'd always said
he was crazy about the common man. He didn't mean they
had to *stay* common, though. He only meant that they, too,
could be born to poor immigrants in a log cabin in the middle
of howling nowhere between the Carolinas, and still grow up
to be a rich lawyer and famous general and own miles of land
in Tennessee and whole armies of slaves and stables full of
fancy horses. And not need any sissy universities to do it,
either. He thought people should have the chance to grab
up all the public lands dirt cheap and be a success like him.
This was the birth of the American dream, and one in the
eye for the Adamses.

Jackson believed in the Constitution, states' rights, no

---

[5] Except nonfolks like women, blacks, and Indians.
[6] Historians call this kind of thing "Jacksonian Democracy."

taxes, paying off the national debt, preserving the Union, and everyone living simply and thriftily except him.

Congress said *he* could have all the money he wanted, so he fixed up the White House in the grandest style you ever saw. He spent ten thousand dollars in the East Room alone, with some extremely splendid chandeliers, blue satin uphol- stery, and gilded tables. His enemies said it looked like a palace and called him "King Jackson," but his friends liked it. They spoke sneeringly of Adams's interior decor, full of "cobwebs, a few old chairs, lumbering benches and broken glass."[7]

Sometimes Jackson had a thousand people drop by for drinks. Suppers were served on silver-plated dishes, with turkeys and fish and canvasback ducks, partridges, cold chicken "interlaid with slices of tongue and garnished with salled," "a monster salmon in waves of meat jelly," and more than enough wine and brandy.

He threw out everything that reminded him of Adams and built a stable for his favorite racehorses, Emily, Bolivia, and Lady Nashville, on Adams's garden.

The first thing he did in office was fire everyone who'd voted for Adams and give their jobs to people who'd voted for him. The second thing he did was send the whole town into fits with the Peggy O'Neale business.

"Pretty Peggy O'Neale" was a blue-eyed brunette who made the most of her figure. She was the daughter of a tavern-keeper who ran a popular watering hole, and she met a lot of interesting people that way.[8] She met John Eaton, and married him, and then Jackson made him Secretary of

---

[7] They figured Adams had done it up like that on purpose, so the common man couldn't come in and get comfortable.

[8] Jackson had stayed there himself, and spoken highly of her singing and piano playing. He didn't know anything about music but he knew what he liked.

War. This caused a social problem, as who wanted to invite a tavern-keeper's daughter to dinner, and besides, there was some question about her chastity, always one of our most pressing national issues. Peggy had been married to a naval purser named Timberlake who was away at sea a lot, and of course, a girl does get lonely. Apparently she'd been friends with Eaton before Timberlake had the grace to die, but nobody had any proof and Jackson didn't believe it for a minute. It reminded him of the fuss over poor Rachel. He said Peggy was "the smartest little woman in America," and invited the Eatons to dinner all the time. Nobody else did, though. Mrs. Calhoun, the Vice-President's wife, stayed home in South Carolina rather than risk running into Peggy in Washington.[9] The only person besides Jackson who was nice to Peggy was little Martin Van Buren, the Secretary of State. He had his reasons. He used to go out riding with the President every day and tell him the whole thing was Calhoun's fault.[10]

It was all very exciting and nobody got any work done for ages. It was known as "Eaton malaria." All they did on the Hill was stand around in the corridors talking about Peggy. Jackson called a special Cabinet meeting about her, and said she was "chaste as a virgin" and read testimonials about her character, but nobody was convinced.

Finally in 1831 Van Buren persuaded the whole Cabinet, including himself and Eaton, to resign. Jackson sent Eaton off, Peggy in tow, to be governor of Florida, and then all the way to the legation in Spain.[11] This simplified matters.

Van Buren went to be minister to England for a while, and

---

[9] Her name was Floride. What would you expect?

[10] Jackson was an honest, simple fellow and he always listened to Van Buren because he thought Van Buren was clever. He was plenty clever.

[11] Peggy had a marvelous time there too. She was a grand girl and did funny imitations of famous people.

then imagine his surprise when he found himself the new Vice-President, and Calhoun nowhere in sight.

Henry Clay ran against Jackson in 1832, saying he should never have dissolved the Bank of the United States as unconstitutional, since nobody knew what to do without it. Most of the voters kept their money in the sugar bowl anyway and didn't care. Jackson stayed put in the White House.

He felt that the eastern Indian tribes should stop hanging around underfoot and go West. He told the Creeks and the Cherokees that all the land west of the Mississippi belonged to him personally,[12] and he'd give it to them if they'd go there, but if they didn't[13] he couldn't be responsible for what happened. A lot did happen, as the white settlers were naturally irritated by Indians taking up the perfectly good space they needed themselves in order to get as rich as Jackson. So in the end the Cherokees, who were serious homebodies and loathed traveling, had to be rooted out with bayonets and dragged off in handcuffs and sent out on the interstate Trail of Tears, which was full of potholes and rivers without bridges. Some[14] died on the way of cholera, or cold, or just plain unhappiness. It was all for their own good, but they were only Indians and didn't understand.

The Seminoles, on the other hand, put up a nasty fight, taking unfair advantage by hiding out in the swamps so we couldn't find them. We only managed to capture their chief, Osceola, by shrewdly pretending the flag of truce he was waving was just maybe an undershirt or something he was trying to dry. In the end we gave up on the Seminoles. Nobody much wanted their territory anyway. It was full of swamps.

With Jackson around there was never a dull moment.

---

[12] It didn't.
[13] They didn't.
[14] Well, quite a lot, actually.

There was the Alamo, for instance, where 188 gallant Texans, including the famous slave-smuggler Colonel James Bowie and the famous professional backwoodsman and publicity-hog Davy Crockett, held off Santa Anna and three thousand Mexicans for almost two weeks before the famous wipe-out. Then in Part Two, Sam Houston ambushed Santa Anna at the San Jacinto River and captured him and said Texas was an independent country and he was its President. Jackson said that was fine. It was just the kind of enterprising spirit he liked to see.

Then there was an Englishman named Lawrence who tried to assassinate Jackson, only his guns didn't work right. He explained the incident by saying he was the rightful heir to the British throne, but not even Jackson believed him.

Jackson was the first to decide that a President can veto a perfectly constitutional bill just because he doesn't happen to like it, and he was like a kid with a new toy. He vetoed more bills than all the previous Presidents put together.

When he left office Philip Hone, a contemporary busybody, called his administration "the most disastrous in the annals of the country." That's *his* opinion. One of the problems Jackson left behind was that after paying off the national debt, we still had $30 million from the public land sales hanging around in the treasury. People were afraid it would be a temptation to the unscrupulous, just piling up in there like that. It was a lot of money back then.

On the way out Jackson said, "I have only two regrets: that I have not shot Henry Clay or hanged John C. Calhoun."

They don't make 'em like that any more.

Martin Van Buren

1837–1841

★

When your children ask you where Van Burens come from, try not to squirm and stammer and brush them off with some fairy tale. Just tell them the truth, that Van Burens are not a sickness but a perfectly normal, natural development, and all part of growing up and being a democracy.

Little Matty Van was a politician, frankly. He was our first politician President. He'd had a sort of law practice once, but basically with Matty it was politics morning, noon, and night. In New York he invented the political machine with the "Albany Regency" and made himself senator and governor and anything else he could get his hands on, and then he swam into the public eye just behind Jackson's left ear like a pilot fish.

Jackson was a plain simple frontiersman, and like most frontiersmen he didn't know what to do about problems he couldn't shoot. It's counterproductive to shoot voters because they can't vote dead except in Boston and Philadelphia, so Matty took over for him and invented modern politics. He invented speeches, rallies, barbecues, smoke-filled rooms, ward heelers, sing-alongs, fund-raisers, leaflets, posters, billboards, decals, bumper stickers, and other basic tools of government as we know it. He was called "The Little Magician" because everything he touched turned to gold, or votes, which are pretty much the same.

Jackson gets credit for inventing the spoils system, under which people who helped you get elected find all sorts of presents under their pillows, like jobs that can make them very, very rich. Well, maybe it was Jackson, but it sounds like Matty to me.

It's hard to see how even Matty convinced the voters he was a Jacksonian Democrat from the outback when he was really a Republican from New York who knew a few things about French wines and which sauces go on what, but that's politics for you. He didn't exactly slouch around in homespun coonskins, either. Somebody described him in "an elegant snuff-colored broadcloth coat with a velvet collar; his cravat was orange with modest lace tips; his trousers were white duck, his shoes were morocco; his neat-fitting gloves were yellow kid; his long-furred beaver with a broad brim was of a Quaker color."[1]

He was nicely balanced out by his Vice-President, Richard Johnson, who always told people he'd killed the great Shawnee chief Tecumseh, and he probably did. (*Somebody* had to.) Killing Indians was every bit as good as being born in log cabins, and Matty was born in an ordinary house and he'd been too busy politicking to kill much of anyone.[2]

Johnson's supporters advertised the future Vice-President by singing,

> *"Rumpsey-dumpsey, rumpsey-dumpsey,*
> *Colonel Johnson killed Tecumseh!"*[3]

You may still not believe anyone could possibly vote for a man in yellow gloves and a lace-trimmed orange necktie, but you're forgetting Jackson. Jackson was still very much the flavor of the month with most folks, and when he said, "Vote for my little Matty," they set down their jugs and laced up their boots and did so.

Being nice to Peggy Eaton had been a good idea. Van Buren was full of good ideas. Oh, some people sneered—

---

[1] His enemies accused him of wearing corsets. They didn't say how they knew.

[2] When he was running the Senate during Jackson's second term, he always wore a brace of pistols, because of the slavery discussions, but the record shows he shot few, if any, senators.

[3] In case you thought poetry had been languishing since John Quincy.

Calhoun said, "He is not of the race of the lion or the tiger; he belongs to the lower order, the fox"—but you'll notice Calhoun wasn't President and Van Buren was.

When Matty walked into the White House he stepped smack into the Panic of '37, caused by various factors too financial to discuss. Banks and businesses closed down and people lost all their money and rioted for bread in the streets, and even Van Buren had to take notice, though it was rather sordid and not his thing at all. He called a special session of Congress, and it authorized an issue of temporary treasury notes and presto, there we were in debt again. From what people tell me, I understand we still are.

On account of the depression, Matty lay low and canceled the larger White House parties and kept the curtains drawn while he changed a thing or two in the decor. Privately he'd always thought Jackson's taste a bit on the garish side, and also Jackson's friends had been hard on the furniture.[4] He auctioned off some old tables and things for six thousand dollars, and got twenty-seven thousand more from Congress for new rugs and a thorough housecleaning. When he finally invited the public in to see, they were disappointed. They'd liked Jackson's furniture better, and besides, there was nothing to eat. Van Buren didn't want to encourage riffraff hanging around,[5] but his private parties were something else again. He had a perfectly wizard chef, and even Calhoun couldn't resist a dinner invitation. Van Buren himself got quite tubby.

He had four sons, named Abraham, John, Martin, Jr., and—his imagination now quite exhausted—Smith. They came to live with him, and Dolley Madison was incensed at the thought of five bachelors in the White House and no

---

[4] They never wiped their feet and they spat on the carpets a lot. They thought cuspidors were sissy.

[5] Congressmen were invited only twice a year.

proper hostess.[6] She sent at once for a pretty niece named Angelica Singleton and bundled her straight over. Angelica decided Matty was too old for her, so she married Abraham, and everyone agreed she made a charming hostess but *still* there were no slam-bang public parties as in the good old days.

People started murmuring disconsolately. Maybe after all, they thought, Van Buren wasn't such a good old straight-shooting Jacksonian. Maybe he was a snob. Maybe he was a sissy.[7] They started calling him "Petticoat Pet." Maybe the depression was all his fault. The Whigs, who were new on the scene and made up of assorted anti-Jacksonians, started calling him "Martin Van Ruin."

He didn't appear to take much notice. He was peculiarly apathetic about actually *being* President, and never vetoed a single bill or seemed to have any opinions except Jackson's. He may have felt that getting there was more than half the fun. I mean, people climb up Mount Everest, but there's not much to do once you get there except leave a message in a bottle and start back down. He said himself, later, "As to the Presidency, the two happiest days of my life were those of my entrance upon the office and my surrender of it." Nobody expects you to settle down and *live* on Everest.

In the spring of 1840 Mr. Ogle, congressman from Pennsylvania, made a speech that lasted three days and really cut loose on how Matty Van's lifestyle was putting us in the poorhouse, and was disgusting besides. He said the White House "glitters with all imaginable luxuries and

---

[6] Some historians insist that Van Buren had had a wife for twelve years, and that she was the mother of the four sons, but he wrote a painfully detailed autobiography and never once mentioned any wife, and surely he ought to know best.
[7] Maybe they'd just noticed that necktie.

gaudy ornaments . . . a palace as splendid as that of the
Caesars and as richly adorned as the proudest Asiatic mansion." He'd heard that Matty'd had a reservoir put in the
White House basement, with a pump to pull water upstairs
for washing dishes and bathing, and he was revolted. He
shuddered at the Greek and/or Roman decadence of the
President lolling around in a "tepid bath" and spraying his
bushy sideburns with a French cologne called *"Triple Dis-
tillé Savon Daveline Mons Sens."*[8]

He saved his best shots for Matty's dining habits, brag-
ging that he, Ogle, liked nothing better than "fried meat and
gravy, or hog and hominy," and wouldn't touch the Frenchy
vittles served on Pennsylvania Avenue.[9] He said there were
"knives, forks and spoons of gold, that he might dine in the
style of the monarchs of Europe," and "green finger cups,
in which to wash his pretty, tapering, soft, white lily fingers."[10]

Van Buren's people said he'd actually cost the government less than any other President, and I seem to remember
those spoons from Mrs. Monroe's reign, but no matter. It
was a humdinger of a speech.

Matty'd beaten Harrison in '36, and in '40 Harrison beat
him. That's politics for you. Matty got along famously with
the new man. A good politician gets along famously with
everyone.

In '48 he ran for President again on the Free-Soil ticket,
just to keep his hand in, and didn't carry a state. Oh, well.

Matty's home was in Kinderhook, New York, and some
of his very best friends had always called him "Old Kinder-

---

[8] I don't know how he'd know, and I can't *imagine* how he
pronounced it.

[9] Who'd asked him to?

[10] It seems clear Ogle had a mole in the kitchen, and possibly
another in the bathroom.

hook." So back when Jackson was still top dog, the initials "O.K." started turning up here and there. They stood for Old Kinderhook, and got to be kind of an inside joke among the Jacksonians. The Whigs couldn't figure it out, so they said, in a sneering sort of way, that they probably stood for the way Jackson would spell "all correct," and this got to be an inside joke among the Whigs. For some reason a lot of people took it seriously, including people who write dictionaries and ought to know better.[11]

---

[11] It's true Jackson couldn't spell for shucks, but *nobody* has ever spelled "all correct" as "oll korrect."

William Henry Harrison

1841–1841

★

The election of 1840 was marvelous fun. Nobody had any sort of platform or mentioned any issues,[1] they just partied the whole time.

Harrison the Whig had been the hero of the Battle of Tippecanoe, in which he killed numerous Indians. He'd also liberated a lot of land from Indians who probably wouldn't have known what to do with it anyway, so he was a strong candidate right from the start.[2] He ran with a Virginia pol named John Tyler, and the Whigs went around chanting, "Tippecanoe and Tyler too," and calling Van Buren a pantywaist.

A Democratic newspaper made the mistake of saying that all Harrison wanted in life was a two-thousand-dollar pension, plenty of hard cider, and a log cabin. The Whigs were naturally delighted and set about selling Harrison as yet another barefoot boy from the backwoods. They claimed that he'd been *born* in a log cabin, which doubled his qualifications and made him the man to beat.

Harrison was born in a perfectly lovely red brick house[3] on his family's Berkeley Plantation on the James River in Virginia, but it seems there really was a log cabin on the premises. I assume it contained the usual rubbish—broken lawn mowers, empty paint cans, wasp nests, mason jars with spiders in them, rusty hedge clippers, mice—and it was no place to go to be born. Harrison didn't actually *say* he was born in it, but he didn't say he wasn't, either. He just smiled.

The Whigs got up parades with floats carrying log cabins

---

[1] There was only one issue all this time, but it wasn't a good idea to mention it.

[2] He hadn't done much lately, except lose to Van Buren. He said himself, "I am the clerk of the Court of Common Pleas of Hamilton County at your service. . . . Some folks are silly enough to have formed a plan to make a President of the United States out of this Clerk and Clod Hopper."

[3] Some go so far as to call it a mansion.

and barrels of hard cider, and wore log-cabin badges and sang log-cabin songs and poured rivers of hard cider down the throats of prospective voters. They sang,

"Let Van from his coolers of silver drink wine
And lounge on his cushioned settee.
Our man on his buckeye bench can recline;
Content with hard cider is he."

Harrison thought hard cider was nasty, and his running mate, Tyler too, was known to have an extremely sound wine cellar and read poetry and play the violin, but no one took the least notice. The best the Democrats could think of was to send Vice-President Johnson out to run around in a red shirt he said he'd ripped from Tecumseh's body after he killed him. It was good but not good enough.

At his inauguration Harrison stood out there in one of those freezing northeasterly March winds with lashings of rain and spoke for two solid hours.[4] Naturally he caught a dreadful cold, just as his mother could have warned him, and so did everyone else who had to hang around till he finished.[5]

There's a charming tale that while he was in the White House, he did his own shopping and carried the groceries home in a basket. Maybe he said he was going to, but he can't have done it often. His cold wasn't getting any better.[6] Besides, the job hunters were driving him crazy morning, noon, and night. Job hunters were a major headache for early Presidents, and lurked on the stairways and hid in the linen

---

[4] He felt it was the chance of a lifetime.

[5] His wife stayed home in Ohio. She thought he was an old fool to want to be President anyway.

[6] He was sixty-eight years old and should have known enough to take two aspirin and stay in bed.

closet and sprang out brandishing their resumes. They were everywhere and there was no dodging them.

By the end of March he'd developed pneumonia and on April fourth he died, muttering and flailing away at imaginary job hunters.

In his portrait he has the anxious, strangled look of a man trying to swallow a good-sized goldfish, but he might have made a splendid President just the same. Thirty-one days isn't much to go on, not when a person has a rotten cold the whole time.

There is one worrying story, though. When he was a general in the War of 1812 he went to Washington to ask Madison something or other, and Madison then sent him on back to join his troops. Later Dolley happened to mention that Harrison would be at her party that night, and Jemmy said, "But he should be thirty or forty miles on his way west by now." She said, "I laid my command on him, and he is too gallant a man to disobey me." "We shall soon see whose orders he obeys,"[7] said Jemmy, and they soon saw.

Harrison danced the night away and had a heavenly time, but I ask you, what kind of future President would rather dance than shoot Indians?[8]

---

[7] Isn't it amazing how these intimate dialogues get all over town?

[8] Assuming we believe the story to begin with. There are days when I hardly believe anything anymore.

John Tyler

1841–1845

★

According to some gossip that's making the rounds, when people came to Williamsburg to tell Tyler he was President, they found him down on his knees playing marbles. They felt this was frivolous and inappropriate to the gravity of the occasion.

Tyler had eight children at the moment, and if he was playing marbles with the younger ones, which was definitely not the custom in 1841, then he was ahead of his day and a pioneer in the quality-time concept and a fine fellow. On the other hand, if he was playing marbles all by himself because he couldn't think of anything more vice-presidential to do, then it wasn't very statesmanlike of him.[1] The gossip doesn't specify.

Tyler was a fifty-one-year-old Virginia gentleman of the tobacco-planting kind, and he'd been governor of Virginia like his daddy before him, and a congressman and a senator, but he doesn't look like much of a marble-player. He has a long bony nose in a long bony face with the eyes set a bit too high in it, making you think of a sheep's skull left out bleaching in the sands.[2]

He had a spot of trouble taking over from Harrison. It was the first time it had happened, and nobody was quite sure whether the Vice-President turned into a real President or stayed strictly ornamental.[3] Tyler insisted he was real, and tried to prove it by vetoing bills left and right, especially anything to do with federal improvements like harbors and canals and things, being a state's righter, and anything at all to do with banks. He didn't even want to *think* about banks.

Well, a lot of people felt he went too far. He was supposed to be a Whig, but even the Whigs felt he went too far.

---

[1] You never caught the Adamses playing marbles, did you?
[2] Don't forget all those children, though.
[3] They called him "His Accidency."

Congress said it was "executive usurpation"[4] and wanted to impeach him. They even made him pay the White House heat and light bills himself. The only reason he was around to begin with was that "Tyler too" had had such a fine ring with "Tippecanoe"; two syllables, you know, accent on the first, and the "T." It was perfect at the time but not good enough to veto bills with.

The very sight of Tyler made John Quincy Adams feel sick all over. He wrote, "Tyler is a political sectarian of the slave-driving, Virginian, Jeffersonian school, principled against all improvement, with all the interests and passions and vices of slavery rooted in his political and moral constitution."

He'd had a nice Whig Cabinet to begin with—Clay and Daniel Webster had picked it out for Harrison, with Webster as Secretary of State—but they started quitting on him. They thought he'd follow their example and quit too, but it never occurred to him. He just replaced them with Democrats.[5]

Pretty soon he could hardly even find anyone to do lunch with him. His wife, Letitia, stayed in her room. Some first ladies stayed in their room from pure cussedness, but Letitia had had a stroke and was partly paralyzed and couldn't help it. Presently she died.

One fine day in 1844, Tyler and a whole gang of Cabinet members, senators, diplomats, and fair ladies were cruising down the Potomac on the brand-new frigate *Princeton* when one of its twelve-inch guns exploded. A couple of Cabinet members and a former state senator bit the dust, and the state senator's daughter, Julia Gardiner, was flung into Tyler's arms with a force that would have flattened a lesser

---

[4] They'd said that about Jackson, too, but Jackson just laughed.
[5] He hoped the Democrats would nominate him for a term of his own. Fat chance.

man.[6] So Tyler replaced the Cabinet members with some more Democrats and married Julia.

Julia was five years younger than Tyler's oldest daughter and very pretty, with an hourglass figure that was much admired before she had seven more little Tylers, for a grand Tyler total of fifteen. In the White House she queened it up considerably, with a dozen maids of honor and all sorts of folderol, and had Tyler dancing waltzes and polkas till the small hours.[7] It was Julia's idea to have the band play "Hail to the Chief" whenever he poked his sheep's face into the room. It gave the band something to do besides sample the punch, and it still does.

John Quincy said Tyler and his bride were the laughing-stock of the whole town, and Tyler's original eight children went home to Virginia and had no comment for the press, but Dolley Madison, who was seventy-five and fit as a fiddle, thought it was just like the good old days.

Tyler has been called obstinate, commonplace, and narrow-minded by those who remember to mention him at all, but he wasn't all bad. Charles Dickens stopped by to visit him and said he was "unaffected, gentlemanly and agreeable." And after all, who established the United States Weather Bureau so we could start having weather like other countries? Who stamped out Dorr's Rebellion in Rhode Island so hard Dorr was sorry he even thought of it? And don't forget it was Tyler who first noticed that Hawaii is actually in our hemisphere, like Guatemala and Brazil and so on, and therefore covered by the Monroe Doctrine and nobody's business but ours. He even straightened out the fuss over where Canada stopped and Maine started, a problem long

---

[6] Some insist they were nowhere near each other, and only got cozy later while he hung around consoling her on her father's death, but that version lacks dramatic clout.

[7] He felt like a kid again.

obscured by thick woods, irascible lumberjacks, and horrible little stinging blackflies. And just before he left office, he signed the bill annexing Texas so it wouldn't keep floating loose.

After he finished out Harrison's term, nobody wanted to see him again, ever, so he went home to Virginia to have some more children, and eventually seceded and got elected to the Confederate Congress.

No, he didn't free *his* slaves in his will either, and I wish you'd stop asking. Who do you think was going to pick up after those fifteen children, for heaven's sake? I'll tell you who freed his slaves. Robert E. Lee did, that's who, and he didn't wait till he was dead to do it, either, and now I don't want to hear another *word*.

James Polk

1845–1849

★

James Polk was not much fun and neither was Sarah. They had no sense of humor. They were religious and didn't drink, or dance, or play cards, or have children. They never went out and never entertained if they could possibly help it. Sarah's receptions were so genteel that she not only didn't serve punch, she didn't serve anything to eat either. There was nothing to do but stand around, or slip across the park to Dolley Madison's instead.

At the inaugural ball, when the Polks walked in the dancing and music stopped and for two solid hours you could hear a pin drop. Then they went away and the party resumed.

They worked hard. They put in twelve- or fourteen-hour days for four whole years, locked up together in the office, scribble, scribble, scribble. Polk said, "I prefer to supervise the whole operations of the Government myself rather than entrust the public business to subordinates, and this makes my duties very great." He was disgusted with his Cabinet, who frivoled away untold hours eating, sleeping, etc., so he and Sarah did all their work and everyone else's too.[1] No one knows why. Plenty of Presidents don't seem to do any work at all. Coolidge made it a rule never to work more than four hours a day, and I could name others who scarcely set foot in the office and things seemed to go along just as well or maybe better.

James and Sarah took it seriously. They did everything but wash the dishes.[2]

Polk always needed a haircut badly and looked a bit weedy (he thought he'd seem bigger if he bought his suits a size

---

[1] Their Vice-President was George M. Dallas. They didn't let him do *anything*.

[2] Sarah was a dreadful housewife. Sometimes when people came to dinner there were no napkins on the table. She never noticed.

too large),[3] but he was considered attractive enough, at least when he took office.[4] Sarah was said to be a raven-haired knockout with a creamy skin, but the hairstyle of the day didn't do a thing for her, or anyone else either—you parted it in the middle and slicked it down to the ears and then let it collapse in a drizzle of ringlets. Her clothes were "rich but chaste."

No one was quite sure how Polk got to be President, except that it had a lot to do with Andrew Jackson,[5] and also with Sarah, whose idea it seems to have been. He was nominated on the ninth ballot, and people went around saying *"Who?"* They'd never heard of Polk, and wondered whatever happened to people they had heard of, like Buchanan, Van Buren, Johnson, Cass, and Calhoun.

Actually Polk had been right there in Congress for fourteen years, and Speaker from '35 till '39, but he was busy working and not the sort of fellow who gets famous.

He'd always been serious-minded. He was born in a dismal-looking shed near Pineville, North Carolina, and it warped his outlook. Later he majored in math, back when nobody fun majored in math, and graduated at the head of his class. His classmates didn't cheer because they'd never heard of him either.

He beat Clay, but that doesn't say much. So did everyone else in town.

Right from the start he was a real-estate President. He said Oregon was really ours, because Lewis and Clark had spent the whole winter of 1805–06 there. Besides, in 1834 a couple of bird-watchers had gone out with an expedition

---

[3] It didn't work. Someone called him "the merest tangible fraction of a President."

[4] Four years later he looked just *awful.*

[5] He was still Old Hickory. He tried to get people to call Polk "Young Hickory," but it didn't fit, somehow.

and come back to write about how nice the birds were there. England said it was hers because her Hudson's Bay Company had been cheating the Indians there for simply ages. We won.[6] Many people didn't care much one way or the other. It was rainy and infested with Nez Percés, but the salmon fishing was first-rate.

Then Polk said Texas belonged to us too, and maybe California and New Mexico and some other places he'd think of in a minute.

The idea of all this suburban sprawl had everyone cranky and irritable, and there were fistfights and occasional gunfire in Congress. People worried about whether the new places would be slave and vote with the South, or not and not. Besides, getting Texas looked like war with Mexico, who thought it was theirs.

Polk didn't really want to fight Mexico because he was trying to cut a deal with them on California, but it wasn't easy. They kept having juntas and military takeovers and new leaders so fast that Sarah never knew which one to write to about it. So in the meantime he sent Zachary Taylor and some of the boys down to the Texas/Mexico border, just to keep an eye on it and make sure it stayed put, and shoot beer cans and hang out. Naturally there was some scuffling back and forth[7] and some people got hurt. Polk said that the "cup of forbearance has been exhausted," and there we were at war.

The generals in charge of Mexico were very stuck on themselves and went around saying that *they* were aristocrats in fancy uniforms and *we* were just a bunch of farmers in dirty overalls. For farmers, our boys did okay, thanks to the old American custom of playing around with guns. When they shot you, you stayed shot. It served some people right.

---

[6] That's what "54-40 or Fight" was all about.
[7] You know how these things happen.

For a long time Polk kept telling himself we were only fighting to defend American soil, but we weren't. Any fool could see we had both feet in Mexico,[8] and virtuous people started calling it aggression. Abraham Lincoln was in Congress and said we shouldn't be acting like that, and John Quincy Adams was in Congress too and jumped up to complain and keeled over and died.[9] Thoreau refused to pay taxes for the war and went to jail. The next morning his aunt came down and paid them for him, and he went right home and wrote *Civil Disobedience.*

Meanwhile, back in Mexico, our stout senior generals were Winfield ("Old Fuss and Feathers") Scott and Zachary ("Old Rough and Ready") Taylor. They'd brought along a star-studded cast of extras, too — Robert E. Lee, George McClellan, Ulysses S. Grant, Matthew Perry, and much, much more.

Taylor scored a rousing victory at Buena Vista, emerging a shoo-in for the next President. Then Scott whipped Santa Anna[10] at Veracruz and struck off cross-country for Mexico City. Like many subsequent tourists, a lot of his men didn't feel very well,[11] but Scott pressed on and knocked off the capital and it was all over.

A fellow named Trist negotiated the treaty. The Mexicans got to keep their serapes and a couple of cacti. We got Texas. And New Mexico. And upper California, later subdivided into California, Arizona, Nevada, Utah, and most of Colorado and Wyoming. We paid $15 million for the package.[12] Polk was cross and fired Trist—he'd wanted northern

---

[8] You could tell by the dysentery.

[9] Well, he was eighty, and there were plenty of Adamses left.

[10] Remember the Alamo? He was back. Don't ask.

[11] All told, we lost 1,721 in battle and 11,155 from diarrhea.

[12] Nowadays you could hardly get even *Nevada* for $15 million. It's criminal what's happened to real estate.

Mexico too—but people were bored with it all and made him sign the treaty.

Polk was a wreck. Wars are hard work. People tried to talk him into taking a few days on the Chesapeake, to swim and eat "soft crabs and oysters," but he just waved them away and went on working.

Historian Page Smith calls him "a petty, conniving, irascible, small-spirited man." Historian Bernard De Voto says, "Polk's mind was rigid, narrow, obstinate, far from first-rate."

Maybe so, but imagine how flat life would be without Texas and California. Imagine John Wayne in Connecticut. Imagine Lyndon Johnson in New Jersey. Now, I ask you.

Polk tottered out of the White House and was dead in three months. Sarah was made of sterner stuff. She was last heard from at eighty-eight, and she's probably still around somewhere, working like a dog all day and banging on the neighbors' doors all night to make them stop that dancing in there.

Zachary Taylor

1849–1850

★

One of the problems with running Taylor was that he didn't belong to any party and had never voted for anyone at all. He thought all politicians were pond scum. He said, "The idea that I should become President seems to me too visionary to require a serious answer. It has never entered my head, nor is it likely to enter the head of any sane person."

Another problem was that he wouldn't pay postage due on his mail. When the Whigs picked him anyway, in early June, they wrote him a letter about it, but it came with ten cents due so he sent it back unopened. Some sources say it was July before he found out, and by then it was way too late to say no.

A third problem was that as a candidate he refused to answer any questions whatsoever or offer any opinions on matters of state.[1] You'd think this would discourage voters, but no. They thought he had hidden depths.

The Whigs had picked Taylor over Webster or Clay, who were only statesmen and not war heroes. The Democrats picked Lewis Cass, who wore a red wig that didn't fit. The Free-Soilers[2] went for a rerun of Van Buren, costarring John Quincy Adams's son Charles Francis.[3] They sang,

> *"He who'd vote for Zacky Taylor*
> *Needs a keeper or a jailer,*
> *And he who for Cass can be*
> *Is a Cass without the C."*

It was clever but it didn't work.

Taylor was plump and bowlegged, with curly sideburns

---

[1] He may not have had any. He'd been in the army for forty years.

[2] Formerly the Barnburners. Are you following this?

[3] Walt Whitman got fired from the *Brooklyn Eagle* for supporting Van Buren. This gave him some free time to write *Leaves of Grass*.

and a battered straw hat that looked as if he'd found it in the trash. Besides, he was walleyed, so that he seemed to be gazing off in two directions at once. This can be disconcerting. He tried to hide it by half closing the wandering eye when he was talking to you up close.[4] He'd never gone to college, but then, neither did Washington, Jackson, Van Buren, Fillmore, Lincoln, Cleveland, or Truman. Andrew Johnson never even got to kindergarten; his wife taught him to read and write. It makes you wonder.

As President, Old Rough and Ready couldn't seem to find any clean shirts and he chewed tobacco pretty much all the time, but neatly. A visitor observed with admiration that he "never missed the cuspidor once, or put my person in any jeopardy." Out on the lawn, his war-horse, Old Whitey, ambled around eating grass and looking a little like his owner. He needed brushing. Tourists pulled hairs from his tail for souvenirs but he didn't mind.

On the whole, Taylor was pretty sensible, for a general. In his first address to Congress he said that the African slave trade should be abolished,[5] and somebody ought to build a railroad across the country, and there should be a Department of Agriculture. He closed by urging people not to talk about slavery—"abstain from the introduction of those exciting topics of a sectional character," he said, deftly avoiding the S word.[6]

Just then a lot of people were on their way to California. They didn't want to get into the movies, they wanted gold, and lived in places with picturesque names like Grub Gulch and Red Dog and spent the day sloshing the creek bottom

---

[4] That can be disconcerting too.

[5] He didn't say *slaves* should be abolished. He had over one hundred of them on his cotton plantation down home.

[6] Naturally nobody abstained. It was *the* hot topic, and senators went right on punching each other on the Senate floor and brandishing revolvers.

back and forth in a washbasin. Pretty soon there were so many people out there that they decided to be a state, and Taylor agreed. They drew up a constitution saying there wouldn't be any slavery, which made the South mad, especially South Carolina, which was always flying off the handle about something or other and stamping out of the room in a snit.

Some people think Taylor was wishy-washy on the North/ South thing, but he did say he would personally lead the army against any state that tried to secede, and instantly hang any rebels he could get his hands on. This is a fairly clear policy statement.

Yes, there was a Mrs. Taylor, but she didn't contribute much. She refused to meet anybody or even leave her room, and sat in there huddled over the fire shivering and muttering that the whole presidency business was "a plot to deprive me of his society and shorten his life by unnecessary care and responsibility."[7]

As it turned out, responsibility had nothing to do with it. I really hate to tell you this, but you're bound to find out sometime and I don't want you hearing it in the gutter.

When Taylor had been President for less than a year and a half, he went to a Fourth of July bash on the Monument Grounds. Well, you know Washington in July, and the speakers droned on and on, and Taylor was mopping the old brow pretty constantly. When he got home he called for a lot of ice-cold milk and cherries and, some say, pickled cucumbers, and he really lit into them. One account says his doctor begged him to stop, but I can't see why the doctor would have dropped by just to watch him eat. Probably it was an afterthought, the doctor being mindful of malpractice suits. Anyway, Taylor put away an indecent quantity of the stuff

---

[7] She'd been an army wife for a long time. It takes its toll.

and came down with a stomachache and died on the ninth.[8]

Patriotic authorities call it, variously, gastroenteritis, typhus, and even cholera. Others say the doctors did it, loading him up with ipecac, calomel, opium, and the most amazing doses of quinine while they were pumping out his blood, but remember the doctors wouldn't have had a chance at him if he hadn't made such a pig of himself.

Let this be a lesson to us all.

---

[8] Ever since, a popular superstition holds that consuming milk and pickles at the same time will kill *anyone*. It won't. Only a select few.

Millard Fillmore

1850–1853

★

Many people are almost indifferent to the subject of Millard Fillmore. It's his name. They think if they'd known a kid in school named Millard he wouldn't have been a barrel of laughs, but they're just guessing. Millard was his mother's maiden name, though I admit that's a pretty thin excuse.[1]

He wasn't a bad man—in fact, he was quite nice. He was just wrong a good deal of the time. He couldn't help it.

The only right thing he did was be born in a log cabin to a very poor family.[2] They indentured him to a wool-carder and cloth-dresser, and being indentured wasn't at all the same as being apprenticed. It was much nastier. By the time he finally bought his freedom and got to school, he was a big boy nineteen years old and fell in love with the teacher. They waited for each other for seven years while he clerked in a law office and then set up his own practice. (It wasn't what you'd call a classical education, but don't forget he could card wool and dress cloth, too.)

He wasn't interested in politics until the Anti-Masonic Party came along. At the time, everyone got very excited about the Masons and the Anti-Masons, because a bricklayer named Morgan had disappeared and some hysterical types said the Masons had done him in. In the nineteenth century, whenever *anything* happened the bystanders got together and formed a political party about it. For alternate entertainment they could read the Bible and rub goose grease into their boots.

Millard went to the New York State Assembly as an

---

[1] He named his own son Millard. I can't think of *any* excuse for that.

[2] See also Jackson, Taylor, Buchanan, Lincoln, and Garfield. Cynics believe they were all born in the same log cabin, rented out for the occasion to ambitious mothers by a real estate entrepreneur. This is probably not true.

Anti-Mason.[3] Pretty soon he found himself in Congress, and one day in 1848 the Whigs were looking around for a vice-presidential fellow to run with Taylor and their eyes lit on Millard. They thought he'd help them carry New York. Besides, he had nice blue eyes and a deep voice and was modest and handsome and a Capricorn, and what more do you want in a Vice-President? He may look a bit jowly to you, and it's true if his waistcoat were larger it wouldn't strain at the buttons like that, but in 1850 nobody cried shame to a middle-aged man who put on a few pounds, or told him to count his cholesterol. They thought it looked dignified.[4] It was the scrawny little chaps like Madison and Polk they laughed at.

Anyway, he was a perfectly acceptable choice. Who could know Taylor was going to overdose on cold milk?

In July of 1850 Millard Fillmore found himself President and hit his stride at being wrong. For starters, he gave the wrong answer to the Slavery Question.[5] He thought it was a terrible idea, personally—he'd been indentured and that was no picnic either—but he thought the states were old enough to decide for themselves. He was a peaceable fellow, and hoped he could stop the Civil War from happening.[6] He also irritated some people by trying to enforce the Fugitive Slave Act, under which runaway slaves were returned to their owners like a diamond bracelet or the Steinway grand caught hightailing it up the road. This was not only wrong, it was impossible.

Another idea he had was opening up world trade. He sent

---

[3] It was the wrong thing to be, naturally.

[4] "Stout but not corpulent," they said approvingly.

[5] By this time there was no right answer.

[6] Five hundred thousand Americans died in it, compared to a mere four hundred thousand in World War II, and it cost around $20 billion. It was *just* the kind of thing he hated.

Commodore Perry to Japan to suggest, by means of the heavily armed frigates *Mississippi* and *Susquehanna,* that they buy things from us. The Japanese hadn't spoken to anyone at all for hundreds of years, and they liked it that way. They were perfectly happy alone on their islands eating rice and kicking each other in the ear and having tea ceremonies. Sometimes, for excitement, his nearest and dearest would conspire to poison the emperor, but mostly life just jogged along. Millard's idea was that, with a little arm-twisting, they'd eventually wind up with an island-full of Chevrolets and RCA stereos, and we'd wind up with a vault-full of yen. His whole career was like that.[7]

His other international coup was about Peruvian guano. Guano is a substance deposited by seabirds on rocks and offshore islands and park benches, and people used it for fertilizer. Millard intervened between the Peruvians and some squabbling American businessmen and negotiated a treaty so we could import more guano. Then everyone started using Miracle-Gro instead.

Mrs. Fillmore wasn't feeling well, but she did notice that there wasn't anything in the house to read, not even a dictionary. She'd been a schoolteacher, so she sent word to Congress that there ought to be some books around the place, and got an appropriation for sets of Dickens and Thackeray. She still felt lousy, but at least she had something to read.[8]

Millard had his domestic side. He called the White House his "temple of inconveniences," and ordered a fancy great

---

[7] When the Japanese finally said yes, we gave them a barrel of whiskey and a copy of Audubon's *Birds of America.* I expect they were terribly pleased.

[8] I've been told she also installed the first White House bathtub, but if so, then what was Van Buren lolling around in, a soup kettle? You can't believe everything you hear.

patented cookstove with all the modern improvements and valves and flues and drafts and a clever place to keep the ashes. Even that was wrong. The cook ignored it completely and went right on using the open fireplace and getting ashes in the soup.

In 1852 the Whigs decided Millard was the wrong President and flatly refused to nominate him. His feelings were so hurt that he joined the Know-Nothing party, a group that claimed to know nothing about what it was doing and believed that nobody who wasn't born here, and a Protestant, should be allowed to vote or get elected or have any nice jobs or any fun at all. He ran for President on the Know-Nothing ticket in '56 and carried Maryland.

He still thought there shouldn't be any Civil War, so he wouldn't support Lincoln and his remaining friends stopped speaking to him.

After that he moved to Buffalo, New York, and as far as anyone knows he was happy as a clam there and nobody noticed he was wrong. When his wife died he married a rich widow and got elected the very first President of the Buffalo Historical Society. *They* thought he was a perfectly swell President.

Franklin Pierce

1853–1857

★

Suddenly John Calhoun, Henry Clay, John Quincy Adams, Andrew Jackson, and Daniel Webster were all dead, creating one of those flat spots when the conversation lags and people look around and say, "Hey, where is everybody?"

The Whigs hauled out Old Fuss and Feathers Scott, the last available war hero. He'd been a real rouser of a general, but personally he was a frightful bore and politically he was simply absurd.

Still, he was a candidate, and the Democrats had trouble finding *anyone*. The convention went into terminal gridlock and the delegates got more and more depressed. New Hampshire had thrown in Pierce's name as one of those favorite-son, token-of-respect gestures people sometimes regret, and after forty-eight ballots when everyone was dead for sleep, somebody said, "All right, so what about this fellow Pierce or Price or whatever?" and that was that.

Franklin Pierce wasn't really nobody. He'd been in the state legislature at twenty-five, and gone on to Congress, and by thirty-three he was the youngest senator. He had this wife problem, though.[1] Jane Pierce was a thoroughly dismal lady. She was a religious fanatic who complained a lot about her nerves. She hated politics[2] and she hated Washington, and when Franklin was in the Senate she stayed home in New Hampshire and he had to live in a boardinghouse and eat meat loaf every night.

They'd had two children who died in infancy, and then when son Benjamin arrived in 1841, Frank resigned his Senate seat and went home to help Jane change diapers and keep tiptoeing into the kid's room to see if he was still

[1] He was called "Handsome Frank" and looked like a poet, but it didn't help.
[2] We can't all be Abigail Adams.

breathing. Polk offered him a Cabinet post but he said no, he couldn't leave Jane.[3]

In 1852 when he found himself nominated for President he had some fast talking to do. He told Jane he was just as surprised as she was. He said he hadn't known a thing about it. Then he hinted that it would be nice for young Benjamin to grow up in the White House. She just sighed and pressed her lips together.

During the campaign the Whigs made a great to-do about heroic Old Fuss and Feathers, and called Pierce "the hero of many a well-fought bottle."[4] They said he had run away from his only engagement in the Mexican War. This was a barefaced lie. What happened was, his horse shied and threw him forward so the pommel of the saddle punched him in the groin. Naturally he fainted, and the horse fell down and broke its leg, and Pierce hurt his knee. That's all.[5]

He won the election. (*Somebody* had to win.) Then Jane found out that he really had asked for the nomination and stopped speaking to him. Then in January Benjamin, their eye-apple, got killed in a train accident and she went completely round the bend. She said God did it on purpose so Frank wouldn't be distracted from his duties.

She wouldn't come to town for the inauguration. After the reception was over the White House servants all went away, and there were dirty dishes everywhere and canapés trod into the rugs, and Pierce had to grope his way upstairs with a candle and find his bedroom all by himself.

When Jane did move into the White House, she went

---

[3] She wasn't about to go live in Washington just because Frank was Secretary of something.

[4] So he had a little drinking problem. Suppose *you* were married to Jane Appleton Pierce?

[5] It could have happened to anyone. Alexander the Great, Genghis Khan, anyone.

straight up to her room and stayed there, all dressed in black, and spent her time writing letters to Benjamin and mailing them up the chimney. It got on everyone's nerves, and mostly people went over to Jefferson Davis's house instead. He was Secretary of War, and his wife knew a thing or two about Southern hospitality, which was a good thing since Dolley Madison had gone off to teach the saints to polka in 1849 and there had to be *somewhere* to go for a laugh.

Frank Pierce was the first President to have a Christmas tree in the White House. He was trying to cheer Jane up. It didn't work. He even had central heating installed, but she still didn't speak to him. There may have been days when he thought longingly of the boardinghouse and its meat loaf. There may even have been days when he ducked into the pantry for a nip of brandy. He was arrested for running over an old woman with his horse—the policeman let him go when he saw who it was he'd collared—and I'm not suggesting Frank wasn't perfectly sober at the time, but just the same it's funny no other Presidents rode down old ladies. On the other hand, he does seem to have been the world's worst rider, drunk or sober.

Jane wasn't his only problem. There was Kansas, for instance. Under the Kansas-Nebraska Act it was supposed to vote for itself on whether it wanted to be slave or non-slave.[6] So of course the pros and the antis all swarmed in to vote for their respective sides, and a lot of people who didn't even live there stopped by just to vote. At one point there were two official state governments. Both of them were illegal. Some folks lost their tempers, and everyone behaved in an ungentlemanly manner and killed each other

---

[6] Nobody asked the Wichitas and Pawnees, who used to call it home.

off with giddy abandon.[7] This gave rise to the term "Bleeding Kansas." It also gave rise to John Brown, whose body later got so famous,[8] and Abe Lincoln came back out of Illinois, where he'd been brooding ever since he said the wrong thing about the Mexican War.

Harriet Beecher Stowe had published *Uncle Tom's Cabin* in 1852, and it was still on every coffee table in the North. People who previously hadn't bothered much about the Slavery Question read it and cried for hours and hours.

The Civil War had pretty much already started and was oozing east from Kansas like The Blob. Maybe nobody could have stopped it by this time. Certainly Pierce couldn't. He couldn't even get his wife to come out of her room.[9]

Later on she died and he drank himself to death, some say from grief but I wouldn't bet the farm on it. He may have been celebrating.

---

[7] We were taught to think of abolitionists as kindly, reasonable, Quakerly types, but apparently some of them were quite human.

[8] He was a man of strong feelings and hacked four people into tiny pieces at the Potawatomi Massacre.

[9] Taylor had had the same problem, but he didn't have Kansas.

James Buchanan

1857–1861

★

Many people consider James Buchanan the very worst President ever. I suppose they think *they* would have done better. I suppose *they* wouldn't have let Dred Scott happen, or John Brown, or secession, and there wouldn't have been any Civil War and everyone would have lived happily ever after. Too many Monday-morning quarterbacks, that's what we've got.

Buchanan had been ambassador to Russia and to Britain, and Secretary of State, and he'd tried for the Democratic nomination three times before and finally made it because perseverance pays off, just as your parents told you. The new Republican party nominated John Frémont, as in "Free Speech, Free Soil, and Frémont."[1] Buchanan won, and Frémont went off to become one of the worst generals in the Civil or any other War.

Buchanan was a bachelor. He'd been engaged, back in 1819, to a girl named Anne Caroline Coleman, but they had a spat about something or other and she gave him back his ring and committed suicide. He never mentioned the matter, but plenty of other people did. They said he carried his head funny like that because he'd tried to hang himself in despair and it left his neck crooked. He didn't. He carried his head funny because he had one eye set higher in the socket than the other, and a weak eye muscle, and besides he was nearsighted in one eye and farsighted in the other and when he didn't carry his head funny he got dizzy.[2]

The best thing about Buchanan was the niece, Harriet Lane, that he brought along to be his hostess.[3] She was young and charming and had violet eyes and she was *per-*

---

[1] *His* claim to fame was that he'd once taken quite a long walk in California, and when he came back he had his wife write him a book about it that sold like hotcakes.

[2] Sometimes he got dizzy anyway.

[3] She'd been his ward since she was nine, and they were very close and had long private conversations, and nobody ever said a word about what you're thinking.

fectly healthy. All Washington marveled at how healthy she was. She never had nerves or migraines or locked herself in her room talking to people who weren't there, and she gave such swell parties that even the Prince of Wales came to visit. She liked flowers, and had a nice greenhouse built that would be there to this day if we hadn't set the West Wing down on it. She grew camellias and orange trees and pitcher plants, and made tasteful arrangements all over the house. People were simply entranced. To judge from her pictures she was only average-looking, but she was such a relief after certain First Ladies who shall remain nameless that she knocked them dead. Numerous popular entertainments and songs like "Listen to the Mockingbird" were dedicated to her, and a flower, a racehorse, a warship, and whole regiments of babies were named after her. Sometimes people thought so much about Harriet that they forgot to think about Buchanan at all.

He was a Pennsylvanian, but he thought it was okay to be a Southerner and have slaves if that's the way you wanted it. He even thought it was okay to have them in Kansas, which was still bleeding pretty briskly. (He tried to help matters by sending them various governors and Congressional committees, but the results were about what you'd expect.)[4]

Presidentially speaking, he never had any luck. There was Dred Scott, for instance. Dred Scott was all about a slave named Dred Scott who thought he was free because he'd been traveling around free territories like Wisconsin with the boss. The Supreme Court had a southern majority at the time, and ruled it was unconstitutional for the government to say you couldn't have slaves in the territories, or the new states, or anywhere else you felt like having some slaves.

---

4 Congressional committees never stop *anything* from bleeding. Try one yourself and see.

This was one-up for the South and made the abolitionists wild with rage.

Then there was the Depression of '57. I'm not sure what this had to do with anything, but it couldn't have lightened the mood much.

Then John Brown came East, immediately behind the most menacing set of whiskers you ever saw. He looked like those chaps who reel down the sidewalk shouting strange words to themselves and waving their arms in the air, and you remember a sudden errand on the other side of the street.[5] Not content with adding to the blood supply in Kansas, he showed up in Harper's Ferry to start a slave rebellion by bumping off the mayor and holing up in the arsenal with some odds and ends of people and a couple of his sons.[6] The following shoot-out would make any television crew dance for joy, with Robert E. Lee galloping around on the outside and Brown's men getting butchered inside, and fine dramatic rivers and mountains for background. Brown survived, and got tried and sentenced to hang. It was a perfectly fair trial, and he had excellent lawyers, but just the same, it was probably a mistake to hang him. Ralph Waldo Emerson said it would "make the gallows more glorious than the cross," and he had a point there.

Buchanan wanted to distract people's attention by buying Cuba, but his losing streak held and Congress wouldn't let him. They thought it might have something to do with the slave trade. They may have been right.

---

[5] The smart money crossed the street when they saw Brown coming, too. He said he was an instrument in the hand of God and could kill anybody he wanted to kill.

[6] He had lots. His mother, his grandmother, an aunt, and three of his uncles were all raging certified lunatics, and this might have made some people stop and think before they had nineteen children, but not John Brown.

Otherwise he tried to do as little as possible about anything so as not to rock the boat. He thought if he just sat
still and kept his mouth shut, things wouldn't fall apart until
he could hand them over to the next man and run like hell.

He almost made it.

Unfortunately the South didn't much like the election of
1860. An Atlanta newspaper put it in a nutshell: "Let the
consequences be what they may—whether the Potomac is
crimsoned in human gore, and Pennsylvania Avenue is
paved ten fathoms deep with mangled human bodies, or
whether the last vestige of liberty is swept from the face of
the American continent, the South will never submit to such
humiliation and degradation as the inauguration of Abraham
Lincoln."

Then in December South Carolina passed an "ordinance
of disunion" and marched off waving torches and singing
songs of an inflammatory nature. In January Mississippi,
Florida, and Alabama left too, and then Georgia, Louisiana,
and Texas seceded, and there was poor Buchanan still President, with great globs of the country we'd given him leaking
out through his fingers like a fistful of custard.

Senator Jeff Davis said good-bye to Washington and went
home to be President of the new country.

Some of us have a dim, confused feeling that when states
secede they go away somewhere, out to sea probably, floating majestically off like a fleet of giant icebergs while the
sundered friends and families on either shore stand waving
and hallooing sadly across the widening waters, but it wasn't
like that. The southern states stayed right where they'd
always been. Anyone could see this was going to cause a
problem.

Buchanan went on doing less and less and trying to make
himself invisible. He was almost seventy and may have felt
it had all been a mistake. Nobody except Harriet liked him

any more, and folks said, "Buchanan has a winning way of making himself hateful."[7]

In his last speech to Congress he said, "I at least meant well for my country," but by this time nobody cared.

At his final White House reception he made a valiant last-ditch effort to prevent the Civil War by having the Marine Band play both "Yankee Doodle" and "Dixie." It didn't work.

When the next man moved in, Buchanan said, "If you are as happy, Mr. Lincoln, on entering this house as I am in leaving it and returning home, you are the happiest man in this country."

If Lincoln had had a lick of sense he'd have turned right around and left with him.

---

[7] He didn't mean to be hateful. His nerves were shot.

Abraham Lincoln

1861–1865

★

Believe it or not, there really was an Abraham Lincoln. Many of us get muddled and think he was just one of those nice ideas, like Santa Claus and King Arthur and the Tooth Fairy,[1] but Lincoln was real, and a good thing too, because otherwise we'd have to invent him or, worse, one of us would have to volunteer to be him.

Lincoln is our national hero and everyone loves him. Some people hate their mothers, some hate apple pie, but who hates Lincoln? We seldom even wake up on one of those rainy mornings and ask, "Why Lincoln? Why not Rutherford B. Hayes?"

The answer is, Lincoln is just like us. He's Mr. Us. As *Harper's Weekly* mused at the time, he "illustrated the character of American civilization." We look in the mirror and there he is, tall and strong, honest, independent, uneducated, ambitious but modest, rough-edged but kindly, careless of appearances and indifferent to ceremony, natural storyteller and cool-headed leader in time of danger. It's uncanny—he's us to the very life. National-image-wise, Lincoln hits the spot.

We even like his looks. Us good old Americans are no dandified pretty-boys. Face on him like a chunk of firewood. Character, just like us.

Mind you, we've grown accustomed to his face. No living American can remember seeing a picture of Lincoln for the first time, but back when people were seeing him in the flesh for the first time he was kind of a shock. "Grotesque" was a word that sprang to people's lips.[2] When he went around speechifying, a lot of folks turned out just to see if he really looked like that, and he really did.

He was six feet four inches tall and carried a floppy black

---

[1] No, there isn't any Tooth Fairy. What would a fairy want with all those teeth? Fairies don't even chew.
[2] "Gorilla" was another.

umbrella that wouldn't stay closed and an old gray shawl in case the weather turned chilly. His ears stuck out and his pants were always too short, which made his feet look even bigger.[3] Shortly before his election, a little girl wrote to him saying he'd look better with whiskers, so he grew some and it did help, but not much.

Most of us know a lot about Lincoln, some of it true. Yes, he was born in a log cabin, and later he did try to shoot Indians in Black Hawk's War but he couldn't find any. We all remember his school days, and how he walked forty miles each way, and scratched his math problems in the soot on a shovel, and the snow blew in through the walls and spoiled his homework, but since he said himself that all his school days together didn't add up to a full year we've simply got to stop worrying about it. Think of what *we* went through.

He had a gray-and-white cat named Bob. He grew up in blue jeans doing all those old-time country things the voters love: killing hogs, milking cows, cradling wheat, pitching hay, clearing land, riverboating, rail-splitting, mud-wrestling, and throwing a crowbar.[4] Later he tried running a store, but he always had his nose in a law book and wouldn't wait on customers. Then he tried running a still but he kept letting the whiskey boil over. Finally he got appointed postmaster, and this gave him a chance to read all the newspapers before he delivered them. The mail was always late.

Some say Ann Rutledge was the great love of his life and died of malaria before he could marry her, but his wife Mary said the whole tale was stuff and nonsense. Anyway, Ann was engaged to someone else who'd taken a powder and left

---

[3] He took off his boots whenever he had a chance, because of his bunions.

[4] He was very good at throwing a crowbar. Why does nobody throw crowbars anymore? That's probably what's wrong with this country—kids don't throw crowbars the way they used to.

her hanging around for years waiting for the phone to ring. She and Abe were probably just good friends. Thirty years later the neighbors remembered he was crazed with grief when she died, and it made a good story but nobody seems to have noticed it at the time.

At twenty-five he was elected to the Illinois General Assembly. Then he passed the bar and set up law practice with a chap named Herndon, and drove him up the wall with his messiness and infuriating habit of reading the newspapers aloud for hours. He kept all his really important papers in his hat, and after he had kids he brought them to the office on Sunday and let them tear the place apart. Sometimes he just sat and looked at nothing for a long time.[5] Herndon said his black moods were probably due to heredity, environment, slow blood circulation, constipation, thwarted love, or all of the above. He said, "The whole man, body and soul, worked slowly as if it needed oiling."

He married Mary Todd in 1842 when he was thirty-three. They'd been engaged earlier, but he'd broken it off, and then went quite distracted with brooding and confusion, and had second thoughts, and third thoughts, and finally went through with it, still brooding. They say that while he was getting dressed for the wedding a little boy at the boardinghouse asked him where he was going, and he said, "To hell, I suppose." Nine months and four days later their son Robert was born.

Abe's forebodings turned out to be well-founded, but he would have had them in any case. He always had forebodings. He called it "hypo," short for hypochondria, and was rather proud of it.[6]

Mary was a Southern belle who liked shopping and flirting

---

[5] He got so depressed he was afraid to carry a pocketknife.
[6] His favorite song was a merry little ditty called "Twenty Years Ago," about this fellow standing around in a graveyard where all his friends are buried.

and having hysterics. Sometimes she had migraines too. Sometimes she felt as if hammers were knocking nails into her head and hot wires were being pulled through her eyes.[7]

Americans like to think Lincoln was just a country boy standing around on the farm splitting rails when we all got together and went and got him and carried him off to be President. It's a pretty thought, but actually he was a terrific pol and always running for something or other. Herndon said, "Politics were his life, newspapers his food, and his great ambition his motive power."

When he went to Congress he kept the House in stitches. A reporter wrote, "His awkward gesticulations, the ludicrous management of his voice, and the comical expression of his countenance, all conspired to make his hearers laugh at the mere anticipation of the joke." Stand-up comedy was born.

He was always a great one for jokes and stories. He used *Joe Miller's Joke Book* so hard it fell apart, and wasn't above telling the same joke over and over and over.[8] He had a story for everything. Ask him a question, and he'd say it reminded him of the story about the farmer, or the Irishman, or the little boy with the raccoon. This could be pretty maddening if you just wanted a simple yes or no.[9]

Your teacher wanted you to remember the Lincoln-Douglas debates, and you do remember they had something to do with the Slavery Question, but you may feel they involved the presidency somehow. They didn't. Lincoln and Stephen Douglas were running for a Senate seat, and Lincoln lost in spite of all those nifty speeches and saying "A

---

[7] He called her "Mother" around the house. This can't have helped.

[8] Herndon just rolled his eyes.

[9] It gave him a good out. Later he could always say you'd misunderstood, and the story about the farmer didn't mean yes, it meant no.

house divided against itself cannot stand," though actually Matthew 12:25 said it first. This left him at leisure to run for President and fulfill his destiny as our national hero and an ornament on every classroom wall. The debates had been terrific publicity, with people trudging in from miles around. Fans said Lincoln "stood like some solitary pine on a lonely summit."[10]

The Republican national convention was a zoo. Lincoln cleverly stayed home and pretended not to know what his henchmen were up to. They were running around promising delegates the moon, that's what they were up to. They also packed the house with the noisiest claque on record by printing up counterfeit seat tickets and giving them to all the people who could shout the loudest.[11] This didn't leave any seats for William Seward's supporters and even if they'd been there you couldn't have heard them. It was deafening. Then they brought in some rails and said Lincoln had split them himself, and the cheers were heard in four counties. Cows ran distracted and small birds dropped dead.

After that it was plain sailing.[12] The Democrats nominated Douglas, and eleven slave states walked out and nominated Breckinridge of Kentucky, Buchanan's Vice President, and split the party, so the Republicans had it made.[13]

Many people thought Lincoln would get killed before he was inaugurated. Some felt it would be for the best, actually, while others thought he should just turn down the job, but

---

[10] Others said he looked like a baboon.
[11] They gave them some free drinks, too, to limber up their lungs.
[12] Mary had always had a funny feeling Lincoln was going to be President, but then, most of Mary's feelings were funny.
[13] This was silly of the slave states, since they would have liked Douglas better than Lincoln, but did they stop to think?

he didn't, and he and Mary moved into the White House with Tad, who was seven, and Willie, who was ten.[14]

In his inaugural address he said he had no problem with slavery in the states that already had it, or with the Fugitive Slave Act either, but that nobody should secede, because secession was illegal. Naturally the abolitionists called it waffling and the South said it meant war.

Longfellow got so excited he said Lincoln was "a colossus holding up his burning heart in his hand to light up the sea of life." The *New York Herald,* however, gave the administration a month and then called it "cowardly, mean, and vicious" and Abe "incompetent, ignorant, and desperate" and urged the people to rise up and overthrow the government.[15]

On to Fort Sumter.

Sumter was a federal post right there in the water off Charleston, and you know those South Carolinians, always getting their dander up about something. Some folks, even Old Fuss and Feathers Scott, thought we should just close up the place and say to hell with it, and maybe he was right.

Anderson, the man in charge there, said he'd be out of bacon by April fifteenth and the government had better send some more because nobody in Charleston would sell him so much as a slice of bread. The governor of South Carolina told him, "Let your President attempt to reinforce Sumter, and the tocsin of war will be sounded from every hilltop and valley in the South."

General Pierre Beauregard and most of Charleston with nothing better to do stood around onshore and kept a close eye on the place. On April eleventh Beauregard told Anderson to pick up and pack out. Anderson said he couldn't, really, but his men would be starved out in a few days

---

[14] Robert was off at college and little Eddie was dead.
[15] They hadn't heard about Lincoln being our national hero and everyone loving him.

anyway. Beauregard sent back saying if he'd fix a time for his surrender, then he, Beauregard, wouldn't blow the place into next Tuesday. Otherwise ... Anderson sent back saying he'd surrender at noon on the fifteenth, after they ate the last bacon. This wasn't good enough, and Beauregard sent back saying he had the honor of notifying Anderson he was going to start shooting in exactly an hour, and he did.[16]

All the guns in the area pounded away all day and all the next night. The relief ships showed up in the middle of it with more bacon, but who had time to cook? The shelling went on for thirty-three hours and Beauregard threw over three thousand rounds of assorted hardware at the place. This was hideously noisy and disagreeable but not very dangerous. Only one man in the fort got killed, when one of his own cannon blew up.[17]

So Anderson got on a relief ship and went away, the Confederate flag went up, the rest of the South seceded, and there was the Civil War, which you already know quite enough about. Maybe you can't tell First Manassas from Second Bull Run or even from Spotsylvania, but you remember who won and that's the main thing with wars.

Lincoln never had much fun being President because of the Civil War all the time. It was all ready to roll when he took office, and five days after it was over he was dead as a duck. He had the war, the whole war, and nothing but the war.

He really did want to free the slaves, because he was that kind of a guy, but he had the border states to worry about, and besides, freeing slaves wasn't as urgent a call to arms as you might think. So he said the war was to save the

---

[16] It was half past four in the morning, but nobody could sleep anyway.

[17] Cannon at that time tended to be more effective from the rear than the front.

Union, and that was a big hit. People got all steamed up about saving the Union and rushed right out to volunteer. This is apt to baffle the modern schoolchild, who wonders what was so special about the Union anyway, and if the South didn't want to stick around, then who needed them, and whose business was it anyway? And why was it such a swell idea for us to break off from England and such a lousy idea for the South to break off from the North?

Questions like this do nobody any good.

Meanwhile Lincoln brooded a lot and had nightmares.[18] He saw ghosts, too. Modern ophthalmologists say this was due to hyperopia, possibly connected with anisometropia, muscle imbalance, and astigmatism. On the other hand they may have been real ghosts. Sometimes when he looked in the mirror he saw two of him, one face its usual swarthy color and the other white as a sheet. He told Mary about it and she said it meant he'd be elected to a second term but wouldn't live to finish it.[19]

The question was raised as to whether Mary might be a Southern spy, since most of her family was fighting on the other side. It isn't very likely. She couldn't even keep her temper, much less a secret.[20]

In 1862 little Willie died of typhoid but went on visiting his mother every night anyway, standing at the foot of her bed and smiling. Sometimes he brought little Eddie with him, the one who'd died in Springfield. It was a great comfort to her. So were séances and shopping. She bought three hundred pairs of gloves in four months. Whenever she felt low in her mind, she bought some more expensive clothes,

---

[18] He thought someone was going to assassinate him.
[19] Home life with the Lincolns was a laugh a minute.
[20] Later the question was also raised as to whether she had all her marbles. Robert had her locked up for a while, but she got out.

but she was afraid to wear them because Abe would be cross. After all, there was a war on. She had boxes and boxes of them hidden away in closets, and owed over twenty-seven thousand dollars that she hadn't told anyone about.

On New Year's Day, 1863, Abe signed the Emancipation Proclamation saying all the slaves were free. They weren't any such thing, of course, but it was the thought that counted, even if it did make workers in the northern cities quite beside themselves with rage.

Then he got elected for a second term by telling everyone a story about a farmer—or a Dutchman, I forget which—who advised against changing horses while crossing a stream.

The war went on and on, and then finally it was over.

In the long run the Civil War was the right thing to do because it answered the Slavery Question, so people could ask each other something else for a change, and gave birth to *Gone with the Wind* and some rattling fine songs. On the flip side, it left the most awful mess all over the place, and nobody around to milk the cows or marry the girls. You can't have everything.

Lincoln was the only President to be assassinated in a theater. Modern Presidents don't go to the theater. They stay home and show movies.

People carry on about John Wilkes Booth as if he were some kind of amazing accident, like Krakatoa, but actually all sorts of people had been itching to shoot Lincoln since they first laid eyes on him. He kept a file of death threats as thick as your arm, and it was only a matter of time.[21] Nowadays he wouldn't have lasted a week.

After the funeral many grieving mourners ransacked the White House for souvenirs, some of which took several men

---

[21] He'd had his hat shot off twice.

to carry. When you've lost a beloved President, it's nice to have a sofa to remember him by.

Lincoln's second Vice-President was Andrew Johnson, because they'd thought a candidate from Tennessee would balance the ticket or bring in some Democrats or something. It wasn't one of their best ideas.

Andrew Johnson

1865–1869

★

Andrew Johnson shouldn't be confused with Andrew Jackson, but he often is. No one knows why. He was a Jacksonian like Jackson, but he didn't have Jackson's charm, or anyone else's either.[1]

Johnson believed in the common man and kept telling everyone how common he was himself, and he really was. His father was a gravedigger and odd-job man who died when Andy was three, and his mother took in washing and scrubbed floors in a tavern, and when he was twelve she indentured him to a tailor. He learned to tail all right, but he didn't care for being indentured, so he ran away.[2] He tried to set up in business for himself in places like Carthage, North Carolina, but he couldn't get any customers. There was nothing wrong with his suits, it was just that people in Carthage didn't have much use for suits. When he was eighteen he married a nice little girl named Eliza who taught him to read and write and do simple arithmetic, and after that there was no stopping him.

He moved to Greeneville, Tennessee, where people had never even heard of suits, and discovered politics. By the time he was twenty he was an alderman, and at twenty-two he was mayor of Greeneville.[3] Then he went off to the state legislature, and to Congress, and back home to be governor, making extremely noisy speeches about the common man everywhere he went.

When he was campaigning for reelection as governor, he heard someone was planning to take a shot at him, so he stood up and whacked his revolver down on the table and said, "Fellow citizens, I have been informed that part of the

---

[1] The White House staff called him "The Grim Presence."
[2] His master offered a ten-dollar reward for his capture and return, but there were no takers. Andy always carried a gun, even in bed.
[3] He was the only candidate with a suit.

business to be transacted on the present occasion is the assassination of the individual who has the honor of addressing you. . . . Therefore, if any man has come here tonight for the purpose indicated, I do not say to let him speak, but let him shoot."

Nobody did. Later some of them were sorry, and kept trying to pass the blame off on their neighbors, saying things like, "I'd have done it, only I thought Sam here was going to." Everyone had an excuse.[4]

Johnson got reelected governor of Tennessee, and by this time he was doing pretty well and had eight slaves, but he still made all his own clothes. It was the only way to be sure they were made properly, and besides it was soothing and took his mind off the cares of office. He even made a suit for the governor of Kentucky and sent it over as a gift, and the governor of Kentucky was pleased as punch.

In 1857 he went to the Senate, and pretty soon there was all that secession business. When Tennessee seceded in '61 he said *he* wasn't seceding, and stayed right there in the Senate while all the other Southern Senators went home.[5] In '62 Tennessee got occupied by Union troops and Lincoln sent him over to be military governor.

Then in '64 he turned up on the ticket with Lincoln. Lincoln was a Republican and Johnson was a Democrat, but he was a War Democrat and they'd sort of joined the Republicans and called it the National Union Party.[6]

---

[4] A man named Atzerodt was supposed to kill him the night Lincoln was shot, but he got cold feet at the last minute. It was hard to find a reliable assassin in those days.

[5] He was all for the Union, and besides he was poor white trash and proud of it. He hated the Southern gentry like poison. He hated all gentry like poison. He was sorry to have missed the French Revolution.

[6] The *New York World* called it "two ignorant, boorish, third-rate backwoods lawyers."

At the inauguration Johnson was all of a twitter about being sworn in, and he braced himself with a little nip, or, according to witnesses, two full glasses of nip. He turned up for the ceremonies drunk as a hooty-owl and tried to say a few words and the bystanders had to wrestle him down into his seat and shut him up.

After that people took to calling him "Andy the Sot," but I can't dig up any evidence that he got bombed as a regular thing. One little slip and they jump all over you.

Johnson and Lincoln weren't each other's kind of guy, and while he was Vice-President Lincoln never once called him in to ask him what he thought of the war or the weather or even to tell him the story about the Irish farmer crossing the creek, but then he wasn't Vice-President for very long and Lincoln was a busy man.[7]

Congress wasn't in session when Johnson took over, so he quickly forgave the South and appointed some governors, and they quickly elected some congressmen and sent them to Washington. However, when the rest of Congress showed up they wouldn't let the Southerners come in and sit down, or even use the rest rooms. The Radical Republicans were in charge and they wanted to stay in charge, and they had blood in their eye. They said the states that had seceded weren't even states any more, they were just conquered territories, and had to be under military rule and get punished for a long, long time, and nobody who'd liked seceding could ever get elected to anything anywhere.

It was clear right away that Congress and Johnson weren't going to make a great team. After the congressional elections in '66, the Radical Republicans had enough votes to override Johnson's vetoes, which they enjoyed enormously, and passed the Reconstruction Bills.

---

[7] There wasn't any use telling Johnson jokes anyway. He never thought *anything* was funny.

Old abolitionist Thaddeus Stevens was the fiercest. He thought hell wasn't hot enough for the rebels. He said, "The punishment of traitors has been wholly ignored by a treacherous Executive and a sluggish Congress. To this issue I desire to devote the small remnant of my life." One of his ideas was to make sure all the freed black men voted. He figured that way they'd be running the South and could *really* give their ex-masters, and everyone else, something to cry about and fix their feet for seceding.

Johnson thought the states should decide for themselves about black men voting, which was the wrong thing to think, and that if the rebels couldn't hold office, there wasn't much of anyone else to do it.[8]

There'd been a good deal of confusion all along about what was to be done about the blacks, and were they citizens, or what? Even Lincoln had been confused. At first he'd thought they should all be sent home to Africa, and then later he changed his mind and figured they could go colonize Central America, even though Central America was already chock-full of Central Americans.

It was a messy kind of time. Seward was still Secretary of State, and he bought Alaska, or Seward's Folly, for $7.2 million because some people will do anything to get a laugh, and it was funny enough but it didn't solve the problems.

Everyone blamed Andy for everything. Congress cooked up the Tenure of Office Act, just to be spiteful. It said the President couldn't do much of anything without Senate approval, including and especially fire anyone. So Andy jumped up and fired Stanton, the Secretary of War, and tried to replace him with Grant, but Grant wouldn't play ball and Stanton barricaded the office door with heavy furniture and wouldn't leave.

---

[8] He did think Jeff Davis should go to jail, and he wanted to hang Lee as a traitor but Grant talked him out of it.

Congress decided to impeach Johnson for getting too big for his britches, and disagreeing with the Rads, and not being able to see a joke.[9]

Johnson said, "Let them impeach and be damned!" and wouldn't even go to the trial. He sent some lawyers, who tried to think of nice things to say about him, like "He is a man of few ideas, but they are right and true, and he would suffer death sooner than yield up or violate one of them."

Thaddeus Stevens said, "He is surrounded, hampered, tangled in his own wickedness. Unfortunate, unhappy man, behold your doom!"

Well, they argued it back and forth for two months and finally he squeaked through, acquitted by just one vote, with the majority of the senators voting for conviction.

The trial cleared the air some, and people cheered up and the Johnsons gave some parties and everyone came.

Eliza Johnson never felt very well and sat in her small south bedroom knitting and wishing she were back in Tennessee, but their daughter Martha did the honors. She was a good housekeeper and covered the carpet with a dropcloth for large receptions.[10] She bought two Jersey cows, and came down to the dairy at dawn every morning in a fresh clean apron to do the dairy chores. There were five grandchildren in the White House and they needed a lot of milk.

After Johnson wasn't President any more, he went back to Washington as a senator, and the other senators were distant but polite and never mentioned the little unpleasantness.

---

[9] They even said he'd helped to kill Lincoln, which was silly. He was in bed with a bad cold that night.

[10] Everything was all over tobacco stains again, and bugs were living in the upholstery, in addition to the ongoing White House residents like black ants, rats, mice, and buffalo moths.

Historians agree that Johnson was an evil President because he didn't fight for civil rights for black men, and Stevens was a hero because he did. This is correct because it is very, very wicked to believe that men shouldn't vote, though always proper to believe that women shouldn't, which is beside the point and morally quite different, as you know perfectly well.

Just the same I'd like to see old Thaddeus make a suit. I bet he couldn't even sew on a button.

Ulysses S. Grant

1869–1877

★

In '64 Grant went to Washington so Lincoln could put him in charge of the whole war, and author Richard Henry Dana was hanging around Willard's lobby like everyone else and saw him. He said, "He had no gait, no station, no manner, rough, light-brown whiskers, rather a scrubby look. He had a cigar in his mouth, and rather the look of a man who did, or once did, take a little too much to drink . . . a slightly seedy look, as if he was out of office on half pay, nothing to do but hang around, a clear blue eye and a look of resolution, as if he could not be trifled with, and an entire indifference to the crowd around him. He does not march, nor quite walk, but pitches along as if the next step would bring him on his nose."

Later that day the general had to say a few words at a reception, and blushed all over and couldn't read his own notes.

Several respected authorities claim there's no evidence whatever that Grant ever touched a drop of whiskey. Well, I wasn't there myself, but his dear friends spent as much time worrying about his drinking, and writing to each other about it, as his enemies spent tattling to Lincoln about it, so I don't think we can rule out the possibility.[1] Halstead, who was a bit of a rat, told Lincoln Grant was "a poor stick sober and he is most of the time more than half drunk, and much of the time idiotically drunk."[2]

What do they mean, evidence? Do they want me to break into the Tomb and take a blood sample? We do know that he *quit* drinking for long periods, and it's a foolish waste of time to quit doing something you weren't doing to begin

---

[1] Lincoln liked to say he wished he knew what brand Grant drank so he could send a few barrels to his other generals. He said it a lot.
[2] McClure said he was drunk at Shiloh. Everyone with any sense was drunk at Shiloh.

with. Folks said he'd been sober for ever so long before his best friend, McPherson, was killed near Atlanta, and then he fell off the wagon and got blazing roaring drunk and cried till the tears ran down and soaked his whiskers. (This isn't what you'd call *evidence,* of course. It's just what folks said.)

Anyway he won the war, and besides, when he was in the White House he hardly drank at all, and it's none of the respected authorities' business or mine either.

Grant and James Garfield both claimed to be descended from William the Conqueror by way of his daughter Gundred. This is all very well except that Gundred was William the Conqueror's stepdaughter. Her real father was a man named Mr. Gerbod and he never amounted to a hill of beans. Sorry.

When Grant went to West Point a clerical error changed his name from Hiram Ulysses to Ulysses S. He was glad, because his original monogram embarrassed him.[3] Some people make a big thing out of him graduating twenty-first in a class of thirty-nine, and completely forget to mention that while he was there he jumped a horse over a hurdle six feet six inches high, which was a record, and for all I know it still is. How would *they* like to ride over a six-foot six-inch hurdle? Anyway he never wanted to be regular army, he wanted to teach math and ride horses, but you can't mess around with destiny.

He fought in the Mexican War under Scott and Taylor, and impressed even the Mexicans by riding for more ammo, under fire, hanging down the side of his horse like a Comanche. When the war was over he got posted to some really boring places on the West Coast where he couldn't take his wife and kids and there was nothing to do in the evenings

---

[3] He was easily embarrassed. He was so embarrassed at Appomattox he almost forgot to mention the surrender.

but get drunk.[4] Then he either resigned or got asked to resign, depending on what you believe, and went back to his wife in Missouri. His father-in-law gave him eighty acres, and he built a house and called it "Hardscrabble" and failed at farming. Then he tried to sell real estate but nobody wanted any, so he moved to Galena, Illinois, and tried to sell hides to shoemakers, and he'd probably be there still except for the Civil War.

Maybe he wasn't a gentleman like Lee, but he was a real bulldog of a general and the North was lucky to have him because a lot of the Union generals didn't care for fighting at all and just sat in their tents playing pinochle and sending excuses.[5]

He said he was going to take Vicksburg and he did. The Confederate troops there said they'd hold out till they'd eaten the last rat, and after they'd eaten the last rat they came filing out to surrender looking so mangy that Grant just paroled the whole bunch. He figured they were sick of war and they'd want to go home.[6] Anyway, getting Vicksburg cleared the whole Mississippi for the North, and Lincoln said, "The Father of Waters again goes unvexed to the sea," which was fancy talk for Lincoln and shows he was pleased.

By '64 Grant was running the war so well, with some help from Sherman and Sheridan, that various people wanted to run him for President. They told him he could call himself "The People's Candidate," but he said, "I aspire to only one

---

[4] Or, if the respected authorities insist, *not* get drunk.

[5] Grant said, "The art of war is simple enough. Find out where your enemy is. Get at him as soon as you can. Strike at him as hard as you can, and keep moving on." Easy for *him* to say.

[6] Imagine his surprise when he met a lot of them later at Missionary Ridge.

public office. When this war is over I mean to run for Mayor of Galena and if elected I intend to have the sidewalk fixed up between my house and the depot." This was a very sound plan but it didn't work out.

We all know that nice picture of him at Appomattox, looking embarrassed and slouching around with his shirt unbuttoned. He told Lee his men could take their horses home with them for spring plowing, and he passed out rations for them, and when the Union troops started to cheer he shut them up and said, "The war is over, the rebels are our countrymen again."

It was one of those high points in a person's life. He should have stopped right there, but how was he to know?

One of the first rules of democracy is that the general who wins the war gets to be President, even if he can't tell Washington from Nebraska and doesn't know which party he likes best.

The Republicans got to Grant first, as soon as we were finished with Johnson.[7] His campaign slogan was "Let us have peace," which sounded like a good idea, and he beat the Democrat, Horatio Seymour, so hard nobody's heard from him since.

Mrs. Grant, who was a good wife and a nice lady and perfectly sane, liked the White House and enjoyed being hostess. It made a change from army life and was much more fun than Galena, Illinois. She said it was "a constant feast of cleverness and wit," and gave a party for King Kalakaua of Hawaii. The food was said to be good but heavy.[8]

Grant wasn't nearly so successful at being First Man. It's

---

[7] The other generals all went West to subdue the Sioux and take out their frustration on Crazy Horse, Sitting Bull, etc.

[8] She made her husband stop greeting the day with a cucumber soaked in vinegar and eat a proper, nourishing breakfast.

specialized work and some of us are better at it than others. I hear he'd never even read the Constitution.[9] He handed out jobs to people he thought were his friends, even if they knew less about the work than he did, and when he accidentally hired someone good, he thought it over and fired him later.

As far as the South was concerned, he couldn't please anyone. Who could? He believed in amnesty for the Confederate leaders, which made the Radicals mad, and in black civil rights, which made the Confederate leaders mad. He sent troops to protect the blacks from the Ku Klux Klan and overthrow the elected governments, and the Carpetbaggers took over and made *everyone* mad.

The President of Santo Domingo offered to sell him the place to give to some friends, but the Senate wouldn't let him buy it. Everything was so much more complicated than war that he got quite testy and snappish and wasn't his old self at all. Then the scandals started.

I mean, these were scandals that *were* scandals. Industrial-strength scandals. The Golden Age of scandals. Harding never even came close. The anti-Grant faction claims he was right in there grabbing bribes with the best of them, while the pro-Grant people say he was too dumb to know a bribe if he found it in his bed, and of course it wasn't his fault what James Fish and Jay Gould almost did to the gold market, but just the same, he *was* the President.

Right in the middle of the mess he ran for reelection against Horace Greeley, editor of the *New York Tribune,* but Greeley looked exactly like the Mad Hatter and was crazy about spiritualism and eating vegetables, so it was no contest. The vote was so decisive that Greeley immediately died of a broken heart.

---

[9] Unlike the rest of us, who gather the family around every evening and read it aloud after dinner.

Then there was the Crédit Mobilier scandal, about railroad stocks, and Vice-President Schuyler Colfax was mixed up in that one.[10] Then there was the Whiskey Ring, about tax-cheating, and Grant's private secretary had to think fast. Rich folks bought whole state legislatures as if they were candy bars, and the railroad barons bought Wisconsin, Minnesota, and California. Some of Grant's favorite officials got so rich they had to leave the country. He was always sorry to see them go. He let the Secretary of War resign suddenly so as not to get impeached.

Personally, I don't think Grant made a nickel himself. All right, so Congress doubled his salary and he didn't say no,[11] but money just wasn't his strong point.[12] What was really happening was a New Age dawning.

We'd spent about fifty years warming up for the Civil War, and having it, and getting over it, and now it was time to move on to the next big thing, which was all about money, and business types getting amazingly rich and then the working stiffs getting fretful about it. Grant just got caught out on the leading edge.

He wasn't even all that dumb. He said he hoped that one of these days "the nations of the earth will agree upon some sort of congress which will take cognizance of international questions of difficulty, and whose decisions will be as binding as the decisions of the Supreme Court are upon us." It was a nice thought, and still is.[13]

Of course Henry Adams called him commonplace and simpleminded.[14] He said the very *existence* of Grant dis-

---

[10] Come to think of it, Garfield never really explained what *he* was doing that day, either.

[11] *You'd* have said no, of course.

[12] Later he got swindled out of every cent he owned.

[13] And Wilson told us it was all *his* idea.

[14] Didn't I say there were plenty of Adamses left?

proved the theory of evolution. He said, "The progress of evolution from President Washington to President Grant was alone enough to upset Darwin." Now, isn't that just like an Adams?

After he'd lost all his money and was dying of throat cancer,[15] Grant wrote his memoirs to try to earn a few dollars for the family. Mark Twain published them. They were good memoirs. They were a *lot* more exciting than Henry Adams's memoirs.

---

[15] He'd always smoked twenty cigars a day, and gnawed on the butts.

Rutherford B. Hayes

1877–1881

★

There is no portrait of Rutherford B. Hayes in the Hall of Presidents at the National Portrait Gallery. I suppose they were running short of wall space and figured that if they had to leave someone out, it might as well be Rutherford B. Hayes.[1]

In a manner of speaking he was scarcely President at all. Samuel Tilden won the popular vote hands down, and then there was a bit of hanky-panky in the Electoral College, with some states sending in two sets of ballots, and committees and inquiries and votes found in wastebaskets, which were the primitive equivalent of shredders, and finally, for reasons not entirely clear, they gave all the disputed votes to Hayes and he won by one. This was a good thing as by now the inauguration was only two days off and Rutherford and Lucy were already on the train to Washington, and it would have been a shame to have made the trip for nothing.[2]

All you remember about the Hayeses is that they didn't serve anything interesting to drink, so Mrs. Hayes was called "Lemonade Lucy" and the usual Washington wags went around saying that at her parties the water flowed like wine. This leads you to think of her as a prune, but she wasn't, she was sweet. She had a wide, kind, generous face and a houseful of children and she'd been to college, which was a White House first. It wasn't her fault that the dresses of the time looked more like lampshades. She started the custom of the Easter Monday egg-rolling on the south lawn, and a charming custom it is, too. She grew roses and lilies in Harriet Lane's conservatory, as Rutherford was exceptionally fond of a nice flower. In the evenings she gathered the family and various Cabinet members and congressmen

---

[1] It's possible that there was so little demand for the commodity at the time that nobody painted one. Painters have to eat too, you know.

[2] He took the oath of office a day early, to be on the safe side.

in the Yellow Oval Room, and Secretary of Interior Carl Schurz tickled the ivories while everyone sang items of a spiritual nature like "There Is a Land of Pure Delight" and the ghost of Dolley Madison wept in the wings.

Some say that not serving wine was all Rutherford's idea anyway, since he'd been a big wheel in the temperance movement in his youth and his speeches at the Sons of Temperance meetings were widely admired by people attending Sons of Temperance meetings. Others say that the Hayeses started out serving the customary refreshments but changed their minds after something regrettable happened at a party they gave for a couple of Russian grand dukes.[3] Still others maintain that before his election, Rutherford enjoyed an occasional glass but gave it up to set a good example for the country. We do know that at the inaugural dinner there were six wineglasses by each plate, and they can't *all* have been full of water.

The matter of wine at dinner versus no wine at dinner is the most memorable aspect of President Hayes, unless you count the talk about him and his sister, which you really shouldn't. Probably it was nothing but talk anyway, and besides, what's wrong with a young man being fond of his sister? She was said to be a real knockout, though not very stable. In any event, they put her away in a nice quiet place, and Rutherford married Lucy, and we should consider the subject closed.

Rutherford B. Hayes rejoiced in an unblemished public record dating clear from his early school days, when he was an excellent speller and won all the spelling bees. He often boasted about this later, claiming there was not one in a thousand who could spell him down. He went on to graduate from Harvard Law, and go to Congress, and get elected

---

[3] I'm sorry I don't have the details for you. It must have been some party. You know those grand dukes.

three times governor of Ohio, and become a valued member of the Literary Club of Cincinnati. He was wounded over and over and over in the Civil War. He believed in integrity in government, and even threw Chester Arthur out of his job at the New York Customs House for hiring more friends than were needed for the available chores. His motto was, "He serves his party best who serves his country best."[4]

Henry Adams said, "He is a third-rate nonentity whose only recommendation is that he is obnoxious to no one."[5]

Rutherford B. Hayes had such long gray whiskers that they dipped in his soup unless he drew them to one side like a curtain. Among his decisive actions in the White House were the laying-out of a croquet lawn and the installation of a telephone. He believed in a quiet life, and couldn't understand why the Indians and the striking railroad workers didn't believe in a quiet life too.

The Indians persisted in making trouble on the western plains and providing useful employment for the army, which kept busy herding them from malarial swamps to desolate salt-pans and back again and shooting at them when they tried to get back home where it was nicer, or at least they remembered it as being nicer. The Indians complicated things by shooting at each other a lot too, and refusing to live next door to their traditional enemies. They didn't figure out about solidarity until it was much too late.[6] Hayes said they could be citizens if they'd be nice and stop being tribes, but even when they were citizens they kept right on freez-

---

[4] Just the same, a lot of people were homesick for Grant. You can see why.

[5] The Adams family felt that not being obnoxious to people was a sign of moral flabbiness and mental deficiency.

[6] If they'd learned earlier, you and I would be living on reservations at this very moment, making patchwork quilts and pewter candlesticks for Indian tourists.

ing and starving and dying of malaria, and what's a President to do?

The strikers were much more trouble because they weren't in the Dakotas, they were in Baltimore, Pittsburgh, Philadelphia, Chicago, Cincinnati, St. Louis, and other populous locations. They wanted the railroads to pay them more money, but the people who owned the railroads felt that the less money they paid the workers, the more they got to keep for themselves. By this time the Gatling gun had been invented, and quite a number of people got hurt.

Hayes was afraid there was going to be a revolution, and gathered in the troops to defend Washington and called his Cabinet into permanent session so they could all sit around the table worrying and wondering what to do.

An unsettling feature of the strikes was the sudden appearance of a lot of women no one had ever seen before, shaking their fists and looting stores and shouting about starvation wages. Most Americans had barely even noticed women for a hundred years, and now you could hardly walk down the street without seeing some. Even respectable women started having opinions, and taking up education, socialism, divorce, good works, private clubs, cutting their hair, breaking whiskey bottles, and deciding not to get married.

It was all very upsetting and some people thought it meant the end of civilization as we know it, not foreseeing that soon the middle class would show up and take over and calm everyone down.

Rutherford B. Hayes didn't run for a second term because he wanted to go back to Spiegel Grove, Ohio, and devote his days to prison reform and the education of black youths in the South. No one missed him very much, and after a few years they could hardly remember what he looked like.

I'm afraid I really don't have anything more to say on the subject. I've already said far too much, and if you want to know more you'll have to go look it up for yourself. When you find something exciting, give me a call.

James Garfield

1881–1881

★

arfield was tall and handsome and genial and scholarly. He believed that strikers had a right to strike and black men to vote, but he didn't stick around long enough to do much about it.

I hope you've forgotten about the Crédit Mobilier scandal, because that was a long time ago and you don't want to hold a grudge.[1]

Garfield was born quite correctly in a log cabin, and graduated first in his class at Williams, and taught Latin and Greek at Hiram College. He wrote poetry, too, they say, though none of it springs to my mind at the moment. He was the first left-handed President, and one of his best parlor tricks was writing Latin with one hand and Greek with the other at the same time. Everyone mentions this, so I'm sure it's true, even though you'd think a person would need two heads as well as two hands. It would be mean-spirited to ask just who was watching while he did it; we have to assume that all his guests could lean over his shoulder and actually read the simultaneous passages of Homer and Cicero unrolling from his pens, or at least distinguish Greek letters from somebody's thumbprints on the page. Just because some of *my* guests don't read Greek doesn't mean Garfield's didn't. Education has gone sadly downhill.

He studied law, and fought at Shiloh and Chickamauga and got made a major general, and went to Congress repeatedly.

His wife Lucretia was a scholar, too. She wasn't nearly as handsome as he was, but she was a good wife and polite to his mother, who followed them around everywhere and told her how to bring up the children and cook James's eggs the way he liked them.

---

[1] You also want to forget about that five-thousand-dollar present from the street-paving people. Garfield said himself there was nothing wrong with taking it, and if he didn't think so, why should you?

In 1880 he was elected to the Senate, but his career there was nipped in the bud because he turned up as President instead. He happened to be at the convention with some delegates, and the Republicans had split up into the Stalwarts, Grant-lovers who wanted to run Grant's buddy Roscoe Conkling, and the Half-Breeds, who liked James Blaine.[2] After thirty-six ballots they settled on Garfield instead, because there he was standing around looking tall and handsome and genial and scholarly. The Half-Breeds figured he'd do, and gave him Conkling's buddy Chester Arthur as a running mate to keep the Stalwarts happy.[3] Arthur was an awful sleaze and many people tried to vote for Garfield without Arthur, but it didn't work. It never does.

Garfield beat Winfield Hancock and moved into the White House with Lucretia, five children aged eight to seventeen, and his mother. He was nervous about it. He said, "I am bidding goodbye to private life and to a long series of happy years which I fear terminate in 1880."[4]

He made Blaine Secretary of State, and this made the Stalwarts mad. Every time he gave a job to a Half-Breed, the Stalwarts gathered around in little knots muttering darkly. Day after day he worked his way down the list of jobs. Giving people jobs was what Presidents did back then, and it took a long time.[5] I don't mean Cabinet posts, I mean staffing every two-bit post office and customs shed in the country, and you wouldn't believe the crowds of deserving politicos who jammed themselves into the White House looking for work. You could hardly breathe. Contemporary observers said you didn't even *want* to breathe. The poor

---

[2] Pay attention.

[3] Are you taking notes?

[4] He had premonitions, as well he might. Even his mother couldn't cheer him up.

[5] Poor Harrison had barely made a dent.

man was working hard and wanted to be fair, but people kept yelling at him and snatching at his clothes and trying to trip him on his way to breakfast, and he couldn't sleep nights. He said they were "wholly without mercy." He said, "Some civil service reform will come by necessity after the wearisome years of wasted Presidents have paved the way for it."

Finally it was July second and everyone took a break. Garfield was off to his twenty-fifth reunion at Williams, doubtless looking forward to telling his classmates what he was doing these days, the way people do at reunions, and then going to join his wife at the Jersey shore. In the train station Charles Guiteau shot him in the back.

Guiteau had been asking for a job. He'd wanted to be the American consul in Paris and he'd wanted it badly, which is understandable since it was a fine job and still is, but we can't *all* be the American consul in Paris. Guiteau was a Stalwart.[6] In his coat pocket they found a wrinkled old copy of the *New York Herald* with an article about Garfield giving all the good jobs to Half-Breeds and leaving Stalwarts to sort mail and run errands. He'd underlined the fiercest bits, and it seemed to have gone to his head somewhat.

Everyone thought Garfield was a goner, and Arthur was already testing the mattresses and deciding which furniture to get rid of, but at four in the morning the President was still quite chipper and telling funny stories.

The doctors rallied round and tried everything they could lay hands on to dig for the bullet. The bullet was minding its own business and not bothering anyone, comfortably

---

[6] When the police grabbed him, he yelled, "I am a Stalwart of the Stalwarts! I did it and I want to be arrested. Arthur is President now!" It didn't do him any good, though. Arthur didn't send him to Paris either. His ghost hung around the District Jail for decades, complaining.

lodged behind the pancreas out of harm's way, but the doctors couldn't rest till they'd excavated.

Dr. Bliss hauled in the big Nelaton Probe and shoved it onto the wound and twisted it around and around, looking for a pathway that felt like a bullet track. It made some interesting tracks of its own, and got wedged in the broken bits of a rib and had to be wrenched back out, but it didn't find any bullet. Then Bliss poked around with his fingers for a while, and called more doctors in from all over the country to poke with their fingers too, and pretty soon Garfield was a maze of secret passageways, but the bullet stayed put.

Then Alexander Graham Bell had a better idea. He was so pleased with his telephone that he thought it could do *anything,* and he rigged up a receiver with a primary and secondary coil that he said would hum when it got near the bullet. He brought it around, and they rubbed it all over Garfield, and once they did hear it hum, or anyway, they thought they did.[7] Bell explained to the doctors where to go in and dig deeper and wider holes, and they did, but still no luck.[8]

All this time it was summer in Washington with no air-conditioning. In an engraving of the bedside scene Garfield's mother is lurking nearby with a palm-leaf fan, but believe me, a palm-leaf fan is no match for summer in Washington, even when your insides *aren't* full of unsterilized doctors and probes. In September the unfortunate man asked to go to the Jersey shore for a breath of air, and they took him on

---

[7] Some claim it was confused by the metal bedsprings. Others say it wouldn't have known a bedspring from a bluebell and might as well have been a dowsing rod, though much later the army did use something like it for finding land mines.

[8] The autopsy found it a good ten inches from where Bell said it was.

a special train. They laid the tracks clear to the door of the hotel, and pushed the car along them, and carried him in.

For ten days or so he really did feel better, as people tend to do once they get out of Washington, but then he died.

He was only fifty. It was a scandalous waste of a perfectly serviceable tall, handsome, genial, scholarly President who could write Greek and Latin with both hands at once.

Chester A. Arthur

1881–1885

★

Nobody knows what got into Chester Arthur. He'd always been considered scum and seemed perfectly happy that way. He was the contented tool of Senator Roscoe Conkling, the man to know if you wanted a soft job in New York, and he'd never run for public office, since you didn't need to do anything that strenuous if you knew Roscoe Conkling.

He wasn't even a Civil War hero like everyone else around. He'd spent the war as cozy as a worm in an apple being quartermaster general for New York. Besides, though he always said he was born in Vermont, rumor had it that his mother, not foreseeing the future, had strayed over the line into Canada before she went into labor, meaning he couldn't be President anyway.

Nobody except Roscoe Conkling wanted him to be. All summer everyone prayed hysterically for Garfield's health. Rutherford B. Hayes wrote in his diary that Garfield's death would be a national calamity: "Arthur for President! Conkling the power behind the throne, superior to the throne!" *The Nation* referred to Arthur's origins as a "mess of filth."

Maybe his feelings were hurt. He spent eighty days hanging around waiting and reading the papers and listening to people pray for Garfield, and maybe he took it to heart and repented. He had Bright's disease, too, though he never let on about it, and maybe that helped.

Whatever happened, he turned into an absolutely acceptable, honest President and scarcely gave Conkling the time of day. Everyone was surprised, especially Conkling.[1] Furthermore, he supported the Pendleton Act of '83, which said that people could take civil service exams for a lot of jobs, and keep the jobs no matter who was elected. This upset all the key people, because handing out jobs had been a good way to make friends, and get presents and votes and surpris-

---

[1] He was more than surprised. He was beside himself.

ing envelopes full of money, and pay people for favors and
so on, as nobody knew better than Chester Arthur.

His old friends thought he'd lost his mind.

Arthur was a widower, his wife Nell having died the year
before.[2] He was considered a handsome dog, which goes to
show you how fashions change, and sported the most amazing tuffets of grayish woolly mustachios and side-whiskers,
as if he'd been trying to eat a sheep without peeling it. He
was also one of our nattiest dressers since Van Buren, and
his New York tailor had to take on extra help just to keep
up with the White House orders. Sometimes he called for
twenty-five coats at a clip.

The first thing he did in the White House was redecorate.
He called it "a badly kept barracks," and went to live with
Senator Jones of Nevada and sent for Louis Comfort Tiffany
to fix things up a bit. Twenty-four wagonloads of leaky
cuspidors, battered hair mattresses, priceless antiques, and
moth-eaten carpets got hauled off and sold at auction, and
Tiffany went to work. Everything that could have fringes on
it had fringes on it, and everything else was painted gold.
As far as the eye could see there was red velvet and plush
and floral embroidery, decorated screens, friezes, sconces,
cabbage-rose wallpaper, and enormous painted urns. It was
simply gorgeous.

Then he moved in and started giving the grandest possible dinner parties, at which everyone ate and drank as much
as they could pack in for two or three hours. Arthur's cheeks
got quite rosy and stayed that way.

One school calls him a terrible flirt, while another says

---

[2] By this time you may think that presidential connections
were unhealthy for women, but actually most American
women in the nineteenth century were sick most of the time,
and died often. No one knows why. It might have been the
corsets.

nonsense, he grieved constantly for his lost Nell. The latter cites as evidence the fact that he had the servants put fresh flowers daily beside her photograph, but I'm not sure what this signifies. He had fresh flowers put daily on every flat surface in the house. He grew over a hundred different kinds of roses in the conservatory and sent to New York for some truly astonishing floral centerpieces for his dinners.

Besides, if he was so faithful and grieving, how do they explain Pepita's daughter?

Pepita was a dancing girl, in a manner of speaking, who found she had so much in common with the second Lord Sackville that they had seven children together. One of the children, Victoria, went to Washington to be her father's hostess at the British Legation. Queen Victoria said it was okay with her if it was okay with Washington, and Washington said *it* didn't see anything wrong with the idea.[3] She was only nineteen and a real peach and charmed everyone, including Chester Arthur. According to herself, he proposed, and she "burst out laughing and said, 'Mr. President, you have a son older than me, and you are as old as my father.' "[4]

The White House issued a formal denial of the whole episode, as who wouldn't?

When Arthur's name was mentioned at the Republican convention, no cheers went up. Everyone was still pretty ticked about the Pendleton Act, and they liked Blaine better anyway. Arthur didn't pursue the matter. His Bright's disease was creeping up on him,[5] and he'd had a fine time while

---

[3] Lionel Sackville-West was a bit of a stick, and Washington figured *anyone* would improve his parties. He was described as having "an unusual power of silence."

[4] This left her free to marry her cousin, the third Lord Sackville, and produce Vita Sackville-West, famous chum of Virginia Woolf and all that crowd.

[5] Now we know that there's no such thing as Bright's disease, but whatever it was, it was creeping up on him.

it lasted, with all that good food and wine and pretty ladies, and enough suits and coats to last a lifetime.

Not to mention the shock he'd given Conkling, which must have been good for many a quiet chuckle under the sheep's-wool.

Grover Cleveland

PART I

1885–1889

★

rover Cleveland was elected before television. He weighed nearly three hundred pounds and wore an immense walrus mustache with bits of corned beef and cabbage in it. Orator Robert Ingersoll said he could "slip his collar off over his head without unbuttoning it," which gives you an idea of his neck, and he had a high squeaky voice and some unusual personal habits. I've heard that when he was practicing law in Buffalo he couldn't be bothered to go down the hall and relieved himself through his office window, and once a passerby sued.

People called him "The Beast of Buffalo." He was a bachelor, and no wonder.

He was a conscientious public servant, though. On two occasions while he was sheriff of Erie County, malefactors were sentenced to hang, and Grover put the noose around their necks himself, tightened the rope, and sprang the trapdoor. He was your hands-on type executive and made sure things were done right.

After that he was a reform mayor of Buffalo, and then a reform governor of New York, and vetoed the five-cent trolley fare and became a popular hero. Before you knew it he was campaigning for President, buying beer for all comers in every bar in town.

It was an exciting campaign. The Republican, James Blaine, was a charming fellow, only it seems that while he was in Congress there was a little something about some land grants and some railroads and some dear friends of his that didn't look good, though perhaps there was no real harm in it. On the other hand, Grover had sired a child whose mother was an alcoholic prostitute named Maria Halpin.[1] Pretty soon the Republicans were singing,

---

[1] Some say no, she was a maker of shirt collars. Well, maybe.

"Ma, Ma, where's my Pa?
Gone to the White House, ha ha ha!"[2]

while the Democrats sang,

"Blaine, Blaine, James G. Blaine,
Continental liar from the State of Maine!"

There were only about a hundred thousand votes between them, and it was two days before the authorities would say who won. If television had been around, the dashing Mr. Blaine would have taken it in a walk, and maybe things would have been worse. Or maybe not.

Grover gave a popular inaugural address saying he believed in Washington's Farewell Address and the Monroe Doctrine, civil service reform, fair play for Indians, home, mother, honesty, and no extra wives for Mormons.[3]

His sister Rose, teacher, lecturer, Greek scholar, and feminist author, came to the White House to be hostess. She was bored by the official parties[4] and went back home the next year, after Grover married his ward.

Frances Folsom was twenty-one and beautiful; he was forty-nine and Grover Cleveland. She was the daughter of Grover's late law partner, and he'd helped buy her baby carriage and acted as her guardian ever since her father died when she was eleven. There was talk about a romance with her mother. He called her "Frank." She called him "Uncle Cleve."[5]

---

[2] Senator Vest of Missouri replied, "What of it? We did not enter our man in this race as a gelding."

[3] Many felt this meant he was a liberal and in favor of the workingman, but they weren't listening carefully.

[4] It was mutual.

[5] Look, she could just have said no, couldn't she?

By this time paparazzi had been invented, and hordes of assorted shutterbugs and reporters followed them on their honeymoon in Maryland and listened at keyholes and peered in the window through spyglasses. Grover was furious, but Frank may have liked it. She was gregarious and energetic and a natural-born celebrity. So many people squeezed into her parties that sometimes hysterics broke out. She shook as many as nine thousand hands at receptions and had to have her arms massaged afterward, but she didn't care. She liked it.

The railroad baron Jay Gould is on record as telling Grover, "I feel sure that the vast business interests of the country will be safe in your hands," and he was right. Grover had said he wouldn't do any special favors for big business, but they didn't need any favors, they just needed to be left alone.

He didn't believe in mollycoddling the public. He cut federal expenses by cutting pensions and aid programs. When some Texas farmers went bust in a drought and came whining to him for money to buy seed, he said, "The lesson should be constantly reinforced that though the people should support the Government, the Government should not support the people."[6]

In the '88 campaign the Republicans behaved badly, and said Grover beat his wife. They said he chased her out of the house into a storm. She issued a formal denial, saying, "I can wish the women of my country no greater blessing than that their homes and lives may be as happy, and their husbands may be as kind, attentive, considerate, and affectionate as mine," but not all that many people believed her.

Then the Republicans sent a phony letter to the British minister, Sackville-West, asking him which candidate he liked. Sackville-West said "Cleveland," and the Republicans

---

[6] He could have put it more tactfully.

rushed out and told the Irish, so the Irish all voted for Benjamin Harrison.

Grover wasn't sorry to leave the White House and go back to corporate law and making a tidy fortune on Wall Street, but Frank was. She told the servants to take good care of the place because she'd be back in exactly four years.

Grover Cleveland was the only President to serve two disconnected terms and count as two Presidents, each one weighing a little more than Andrew Jackson and nearly twice as much as Madison, with Harrison wedged between.

Benjamin Harrison

1889–1893

★

enjamin Harrison was the grandson of William Henry Harrison, and I suppose that explains it, though it's hard to see why it should be an advantage. We have no real evidence that William Henry would have been any more effective alive than he was dead.[1]

Benjamin bought a lot of his votes, though not quite enough. Cleveland got a hundred thousand more than he did in the popular count, but Harrison got New York and Indiana and that's what matters. After the election he found out his campaign people had sold all the Cabinet posts for cash to pay election expenses, so he didn't have anyone to appoint and just sat there looking foolish.

He was five feet six inches tall and wore a long flowing beard to make him seem taller. It works out pretty well in his portraits. Back home he used to superintend a Sunday school, when he wasn't busy being defeated in local elections, and teach a men's Bible class. Cigars were his only real interest in life. If you asked him about cigars he brightened right up. Otherwise he didn't. Unkind people called him "The White House Iceberg" and said he had a handshake like a wilted petunia.

His wife, Caroline, was very fond of orchids and painted pictures of orchids on all the dinner plates and cups and saucers. She hated the White House because it was full of people all the time, tramping back and forth to see her husband, ruining the carpets and distracting her from painting on plates. She kept submitting architectural plans to Congress for new, improved White Houses, some of them as big as Pittsburgh and much fancier.[2] Congress refused to build any more White Houses, and in 1892 she died.

The reporters and photographers were so bored with the

---

[1] Some people get the Harrisons mixed up, but manage to lead fairly normal lives just the same.

[2] Everyone laughed except Benjamin, who never could see a joke.

Harrisons that they took up Baby McKee, their grandson, instead. He was a towheaded little boy with a little cart pulled by a little goat named His Whiskers, and for four years the American public saw more of him than they did of their own families. White House spokespersons said Baby McKee and the President were constant companions, but actually they rarely met except for photo opportunities.[3]

Presently the English financial house of Baring failed, and this was a more significant event than you might think and the whole world sank into a financial decline. People were unemployed, and the Socialists and Anarchists came out from wherever Socialists and Anarchists wait when there's no depression. Harrison didn't know *what* to do, but neither did anyone else.

During Harrison's administration the Dakotas, Montana, Idaho, and Washington became states. Some people cite this as evidence of executive leadership, but I'm not sure about that. Sooner or later they would have become states even without Harrison, because the map looked so odd without them.

Harrison's most decisive action was having the White House wired for electricity, which was a progressive step even if it did show up the stains on the carpets. Unfortunately the whole Harrison family was terrified of the stuff and refused to touch the switches for fear of getting fried. They left the lights burning when they went to bed and the servants turned them off in the morning.

Teddy Roosevelt called Harrison "a cold-blooded, narrow-minded, prejudiced, obstinate, timid old psalm-singing Indianapolis politician."[4]

---

[3] Harrison didn't have anything against children, but he never knew what to say to them. He couldn't even ask Baby McKee what he did in school today, because Baby McKee didn't go to school, and wasn't interested in cigars yet either.

[4] And that's only what he said in public.

Well, let me see now. In 1897 Harrison wrote a book called *This Country of Ours,* and the *Ladies' Home Journal* ran it in installments and Scribner's published it. It was all right if you like that sort of thing.

And he was the first President to watch a professional baseball game. Cincinnati beat Washington 7–4 in the eleventh.

I guess that's about it.

Grover Cleveland

PART II

1893–1897

★

leveland II was for gold and the McKinley Tariff, and the Democratic platform was for silver and no McKinley Tariff, but it didn't seem to matter. He won anyway, and walked right into a walloping depression, with millions of unemployed.[1] If there was one thing that got Grover's goat, it was people being unemployed, because it was bad for business and probably all their own fault.

To make matters worse, even people who *did* have perfectly good jobs in the mines or the steel mills or on the railroads didn't like making three dollars for a ten-hour day,[2] and went on strike. Sometimes Grover had to be quite firm with them, and send in Pinkertons, federal troops, the militia, special deputies, etc., to keep them from breaking things. Some strikers resorted to unfair tactics, like Mother Jones and her army of three thousand miners' wives with buckets and mops, all screeching and banging on the buckets and frightening the scabs and the mine mules. Then Emma Goldman started making speeches about strikes in New York, and had to go to jail for a year.[3]

Things brightened up briefly with the Chicago World's Columbian Exposition, which was a grand fair and a great success. Cleveland opened it with a stirring speech about how all these fine things on display proved we were the greatest nation in the world and could teach the rest of them a thing or two about freedom and enterprise. George Ferris reinvented the wheel for the fair. Harry Houdini was there. Henry Adams was there, and spent a long time staring at steam engines and dynamos.[4]

---

[1] No, this wasn't the same as Harrison's depression. This was the depression of 1893.

[2] Remember, you could buy *much* more with three dollars in 1893.

[3] She enjoyed it hugely. She was that kind of a girl.

[4] Afterward he wrote about them interminably. He thought they Meant Something, but they probably don't.

Then the fair closed and everyone went back to being depressed. There were thousands of tramps wandering all over the place, because in those days the homeless didn't settle down on sidewalks and in train stations, they walked around and frightened old ladies. People expected Congress to do something, but all Congress could think of was to keep fiddling with the tariffs.

In the spring of '94 a little fellow named Jacob Coxey got some people together to march on Washington and ask about jobs. He called it "a petition in boots." About four hundred of them started out from Massilon, Ohio, accompanied by a six-piece band and forty reporters. Coxey's wife had a baby, and he named it Legal Tender and brought it along. The weather was terrible, but they kept on slogging. By the time they got to Pennsylvania Avenue there were possibly thousands of reporters and it was a major media event, with Coxey's daughter Mame leading them on a white horse, dressed as Peace. Grover called the cops, who broke a lot of their heads and put Coxey in jail for carrying a sign and walking on the grass, and that was the end of *that*.

There was nothing wimpy about Cleveland when it came to keeping malcontents in their place. He sent more troops to break up the Pullman strike, and put Eugene V. Debs in jail for starting it. The *New York Times* thought this was a good thing and said Debs was "an enemy of the human race," but the Socialists were pretty disgruntled.[5]

A determined doctor managed to heave Grover's mustache aside long enough to look in his mouth and find a tumor. Grover didn't want to worry the stock market, so on July 1, 1893, he had secret surgery in the dead of night, on the yacht *Oneida* in the East River, and never told a soul. With a lot of his jaw gone he had trouble talking, so a dentist made him a rubber jaw that fattened his jowls back to their

---

[5] Socialists, if you've noticed, are almost never gruntled.

familiar bulge and fixed his voice as good as ever, which wasn't great. When he spoke to Congress in August they never noticed, and the story didn't break till he'd been dead for years. It hadn't helped the stock market, though. It was already worried, and it stayed worried.

If you still need to know more about that tumor, the dentist, Dr. Kasson Gibson, kept it for a souvenir, and it wound up in the Mutter Museum in Philadelphia, where you can visit it any time, right next to John Wilkes Booth's thorax and some urinary stones of Chief Justice Marshall's. It's not much to look at, though.

Conservative historians consider Cleveland the most distinguished President between Lincoln and Teddy Roosevelt. When pressed to explain, they say he was honest, which seems to astonish them, and saved the country from protective tariffs and dumping the gold standard, heaven forbid.[6] They say he had a sterling character, compared to a lot of people, and was independent, brave, firm, and upright.

Historians don't care if you look like a walrus and beat your wife and piss out the window. They just care about history.

_____

[6] Please don't worry about the gold standard. Other people are worrying about it for you.

William McKinley

1897–1901

★

McKinley was assassinated by an anarchist. Plenty of Presidents were just *asking* to be assassinated, but not McKinley. He was a nice man, and it was a darned shame because very few nice men get to be President. You would never have heard of McKinley if Mark Hanna hadn't needed a nice President.

Mark Hanna had made enough money selling groceries and running mines to buy Ohio, and he appointed McKinley governor of it, to keep things perking along for his businesses and everyone else's. Hanna loved business more than anything, and he knew McKinley loved it too, because he'd spent fourteen years in Congress jacking up the tariffs to make things cozier for business. He was a staunch Republican.[1]

McKinley loved business so much that in 1896 Hanna decided he should be President. He told everyone to vote for McKinley, while McKinley sat home on his front porch and smiled. The Democrat was William Jennings Bryan the Boy Orator, and he made his famous speech saying gold was so awful and disgusting that nobody should be crucified on a cross of it. This sounded terrific,[2] but since your basic voter didn't understand it any better than you do, he voted for Mark Hanna's man, who hadn't said a word.

All Washington marveled at how nice McKinley was. People stopped each other on street corners, shaking their heads and saying McKinley was the nicest man they'd ever met.[3] His wife, Ida, had lost two infant daughters and hadn't been quite herself since. She had her good days and her bad

---

[1] Nobody knows why Democrats, Socialists, Federalists, etc., are never staunch, but that's the way it is. Only Republicans are staunch.

[2] *Everything* Bryan said sounded terrific.

[3] Teddy Roosevelt said, "McKinley has no more backbone than a chocolate eclair," but Teddy really only admired men who shot tigers, and charged up San Juan Hill, and were named Teddy Roosevelt.

days. She'd also taken up phlebitis and epileptic fits, and nobody wanted to sit next to her at White House dinners, so McKinley sat beside her himself.[4] He took very good care of her, and when she had a seizure during state receptions, he hurried to her side and flung a napkin over her face so no one would notice.[5]

I suppose you're thinking, if McKinley was such a sweet-heart, how do you explain the Spanish-American War, and us being an empire all of a sudden, and taking all those islands from Spain?

Well, it's a long story, but it wasn't *McKinley's* fault. It all began back in Cleveland's time, with some local uprisings in Cuba, which belonged to Spain. High-minded people thought we should hustle right down there and help the Cubans, and business types thought we should hustle right down and protect American business interests, but Cleveland kept the lid on it for a while.

Still, people went on complaining that Spain was being mean to Cuba and we hadn't had a good war in ages and were all sitting around getting rusty. Then it seems there was this battleship, the *Maine,* that had stopped off in Havana Harbor for a rum and Coke, and on February 15, 1898, it happened to blow up. It was quite a blast, and 266 sailors got killed. This is a lot of sailors. You can't pretend not to notice 266 sailors getting blown sky-high.

McKinley said it was probably some kind of accident,[6] but Teddy Roosevelt said Spain had done it and it was an act of war.[7] Some people thought Cuba did it to make Spain look

---

[4] Lots of Presidents would have made her stay in her room.

[5] Well, that's what I'm told. Maybe they were just pretending not to notice.

[6] Later a commission of inspectors said it was due to "an external cause." That ruled out the microwave.

[7] He was Assistant Secretary of the Navy, and as far as I know nobody asked him, but he was always hyperactive.

bad, and some thought certain American newspaper publishers did it to make headlines look good.[8] Whatever happened, it certainly did blow up.

Spain felt just terrible about it, and the Queen of Spain and the Pope and other influentials said they'd do *anything* if only we'd stop being angry, and besides, the new governor-general of Cuba was much kinder than the old one, and the Cubans had all quieted down and the troubles were over.

This would have been fine with McKinley, but it wasn't fine with Congress, or Teddy either. They kept nagging at McKinley until he burst into tears and said all right, then, let's have a war.[9]

John Long was the real Secretary of the Navy, but he couldn't do a thing with his Assistant, who was jumping out of his skin with excitement. Long threw up his hands and went to take a nap, and Teddy sent Admiral Dewey to the Philippines, which also belonged to Spain, besides being a swell place for us to park our navy in the future, not to mention all the trade we could open up in the neighborhood. When Dewey got to Manila Bay he said, "You may fire when ready, Gridley," and sank the Spanish fleet.[10]

Then Teddy made sure the navy had plenty of guns, sent out a call to enlist more seamen, and resigned. He ordered an extra-splendid uniform from Brooks Brothers and started organizing the Rough Riders. He could hardly wait.

The Spanish-American War was the shortest war on record at the time, being before Grenada though similar to it, and lasted from April till August. We lost 379 men fighting, plus 5,083 from the usual other causes, and won all the

---

[8] Personally, I think Teddy did it. It could get awfully quiet just sitting around being an Assistant Secretary.

[9] According to a friend, he "broke down and wept as I have never seen anyone weep in my life. His whole body was shaken with convulsive sobs." I *told* you he was nice.

[10] It was terribly fragile. Just a few little holes and down it went.

islands. We paid Spain $20 million for the Philippines, and they threw in Guam[11] for good measure, and we took Puerto Rico, and gave Cuba to itself on condition that it install better toilets and let us keep some navy there. Then we decided we'd better have Hawaii, too. Teddy said we needed it to defend the Philippines, and the Senate Foreign Relations Committee said we deserved it because our feelings toward it were like "the love of a father for his children."

McKinley prayed a lot for guidance, and God told him he should accept the Philippines as a personal gift from Himself. So here we were with all these islands. Rudyard Kipling advised McKinley to "Take up the white man's burden," and he agreed that we couldn't just set a lot of brown people adrift on their own, getting into who knows what mischief, running through stop signs and ripping the tags off their mattresses. It was plainly our duty to civilize them, and sell them things, and convert them to Christianity. (They'd been Catholic for centuries, but McKinley was a homebody and not quite clear about foreign lands.)[12]

The Filipinos didn't want to be ours, so McKinley had to send troops and spend several years working on what he called "benevolent assimilation." Some historians think it was too bad about the thousands of Filipinos who got killed being assimilated, and the torture and concentration camps and so on, but nobody doubts that McKinley was completely sincere and only trying to help. Besides, if God had given him the place, what was he supposed to do, give it back?

In 1900 it was time to run for reelection. The Vice-President, Garrett Hobart, had died somewhere along the way, so we needed a new one, and wouldn't you know Teddy showed up at the convention in his Rough Riders hat and all hell broke loose? It made McKinley terribly nervous and

---

[11] *Guam?*
[12] Early on, he'd asked a friend where the Philippines were, but the friend didn't know either.

twitchy just to be in the same room with Teddy, but as usual nobody paid any attention to what McKinley wanted.[13] Besides, Teddy had been crashing around being governor of New York and Boss Platt, who was in charge of New York, wanted him out of there before he broke something.

William James called the team "a combination of slime and grit, soap and sand." McKinley sat on his front porch and smiled, and Teddy ran around making hundreds of speeches about prosperity and the Full Dinner Pail. The Democrats dragged out William Jennings Bryan again, who was still calling himself the Boy Orator though he was fully forty years old, and still whining about the cross of gold though people kept yawning and scowling at their watches.

McKinley was reelected, and he was just as nice the second time around, and mellower about tariffs. He smiled and nodded and always wore a clean white vest, which he changed several times a day, with a red carnation in his buttonhole. (He was usually smoking a cigar, too, but he hid it for photographers.)

In September 1901 he went to the Pan American Exposition in Buffalo. As he bent down to give a little girl his red carnation, he was shot at close range by a fellow named Czolgosz.[14] Czolgosz had been brooding about this and that, and bought a gun from a Sears, Roebuck catalog and told a friend he was going to shoot a priest with it, just to show people. The friend said not to bother, that there were so many priests nobody would notice, so he shot McKinley instead and everyone noticed.[15]

McKinley was nice even when shot, and immediately gasped to his secretary, "My wife—be careful, Cortelyou,

---

[13] People are like that when you're really nice.

[14] Pronounced "Czolgosz."

[15] Czolgosz's dying words were, "I am an anarchist. I don't believe in marriage. I believe in free love." There's probably a message in this somewhere; I'm working on it.

how you tell her!" and added that nobody was to hurt poor Czolgosz.

The doctors, who hadn't learned a thing from the Garfield incident, spent a week digging around in McKinley for the bullet, and then he died. I've been told that he died singing "Nearer, My God, to Thee," and I've been trying to believe it. Some days I almost do.

It has been suggested that McKinley and Garfield were really the same President, since they were both Republicans from Ohio, both had been senators and congressmen, both died in September from gunshot and doctors, and both had eight letters in their last names.

There is no truth in this theory, and I'm sorry I even brought it up. Besides, Garfield had whiskers and was all of six inches taller than McKinley.

Theodore Roosevelt

1901–1909

★

We know more about Teddy Roosevelt than we do about most Presidents because he's more fun to know about, and invented the Teddy bear. He always had a wonderful time doing exciting things and making sure they got written up in all the papers. Everyone loved him, except the conservatives and Mark Hanna, who had no sense of humor and called him "that damned cowboy."[1]

The high point of the Spanish-American War was Teddy leading the Rough Riders and whole squadrons of reporters up San Juan Hill. It was a terrific moment, and nobody cared a bit that it wasn't San Juan Hill at all but a small mound in the neighborhood called Kettle Hill. One or two stalwart historians insist that Kettle Hill was a good way to *get* to San Juan Hill, and it was certainly close to it, because Teddy himself said in his memoirs that it offered "a splendid view of the charge on the San Juan blockhouse." Other historians say he was just plain lost[2] and by the time he got to the right hill, it was all over, and a mere handful of five thousand American troops had routed the five hundred defending Spaniards.

Nobody even cared that in the confusion the Rough Riders had left their horses behind in Tampa and had to charge up hills on foot, which isn't half as gallant and stirring except when it's Teddy doing it, chanting, "Rough, rough, we're the stuff! We want to fight and can't get enough! Whoopee!"[3] He trudged up the wrong hill with such flair and dash that it ended up making him the most important person in the whole world. Style counts.

Teddy did not shoot McKinley. Everyone saw Czolgosz do it, and it's just as well he did because otherwise Teddy

---

[1] They thought he was a liberal. He often sounded like one.
[2] He couldn't see very well, even with his glasses.
[3] To make up for the missing horses he tried stealing a locomotive, but it wasn't the same at all.

might have done something regrettable.[4] At the funeral he
could hardly keep from crowing.[5]

He moved into the White House with his nice quiet wife,
Edith, and their children, who took after their father. There
were only six of them by actual count, but in full cry they
sounded like dozens. They were allowed to come down to
dinner with important guests, and interrupt and bang on the
table with their knives and forks.[6] They understood their
responsibility to the press and public and were always doing
fun things like taking their pony upstairs in the elevator,
roller-skating in the halls, and sliding down the grand staircase on trays they'd swiped from the pantry, while the staff
reminisced wistfully about the sweet little Cleveland girls.
They kept badgers, raccoons, cats, dogs, birds, guinea pigs,
snakes, a kangaroo rat, a bear, and the pony, Algonquin.
They brought in friends to help them throw spitballs at the
portraits of Presidents past. Alice was the oldest and very
pretty, but a cutup too. Her father said, "I can do one of two
things. I can be President of the United States, or I can
control Alice." She refused to go to school, and liked jumping into swimming pools with all her clothes on. It was a
great relief to her parents when she married Representative
Nicholas Longworth of Ohio.[7] They thought marriage would
slow her down some. It didn't. She went on being a famous
Washington cutup pretty much forever, and said many
awful, famous things about famous people, and everyone

---

[4] Being Vice-President was even duller than being Assistant
Secretary of the Navy.

[5] Lincoln Steffens wrote, "His joy showed in every word and
movement," and a few days later he "laughed with glee at
the power and place that had come to him."

[6] Teddy's gray cat, Slippers, came to dinner too but had
impeccable manners.

[7] It was a swell wedding. She borrowed a dress sword from a
bystander and whacked up the cake with it.

wanted to sit next to her so they could repeat what she'd said the next morning.

The reformers expected Teddy to be a reformer, because he'd been trying to reform New York while he was governor there, but he said he was President of *all* the people, and could certainly see both sides of this labor/capital business. He believed that people who own mines and mills have rights the same as the rest of us, though he wished they didn't have to make such mean, dirty money, instead of already having plenty of nice clean money like the Roosevelts.[8]

Not that he was *against* unions. He just didn't want them slowing down production with strikes and so on. He stepped into the coal strike in 1902 and said he'd jolly well send in the army to run the mines if both sides didn't come to an agreement on the double. And he dug up the Sherman Anti-Trust Act and brought suits against forty-four major corporations. And he invented the Square Deal, which said that if a brick fell on you at work, the company should do something nice for your widow, and that people who make medicines should stop putting poisonous or addictive ingredients in them, or if they did, they should say so on the label. He even made it illegal to sell spoiled meat.

Unless you happened to be a major corporation he was the greatest possible fun to have in the White House, and people could hardly wait to open their papers in the morning to see what he'd been doing. He invited prizefighters to dinner and staged jujitsu and Chinese wrestling matches in the East Room. He was a pioneer fitness nut and loved boxing, wrestling, tennis, fencing, carrying a big stick, running around and around the Monument Grounds, playing

---

[8] The Roosevelts had had money for so long nobody remembered where it came from. It just sort of ran in the family, like politics and asthma.

cowboys and Indians with his children, and killing animals.[9] He thought fitness was so important that he invented the Rock Creek Test. He took his aides and staff and prospective Cabinet members and new ambassadors to Rock Creek Park for a workout of running, scrambling, wading, swimming, and climbing. The object was to proceed in a straight line through or over everything in the way, including small houses. Anyone who drowned or broke his neck or sat down and cried was a weakling and unfit for his post.

The new French ambassador reported that "it is important to walk straight into a river, or mudhole, and avoid with a feeling of horror paths and bridges." He passed. The new British ambassador failed dismally. He got stuck while rock-climbing, and Teddy had to haul him to the top by his collar, and afterward kept writing to the British Foreign Office saying the man was quite useless and ought to be recalled.

One day it occurred to Teddy that it would be simpler if we could take a boat from the Atlantic to the Pacific without going clear around Patagonia. Since it would take too long to dig a trench clear across *our* country, the smart place to dig was across a part of Colombia where the Americas were only fifty miles wide. He asked Colombia about buying it, but they wanted too much money. Then he realized that the people who lived in this narrow place were probably sick of being part of Colombia and just dying to be independent, and if they were independent they could rent us a strip for our canal. So he sent some warships down there to protect their right to have a revolution if they should happen to want to, and after some prodding they did. (It was sad that a Chinese laundryman and somebody's dog got killed in the uprising, but remember they died in the cause of liberty.) As soon as we'd freed the natives from the yoke of Bogotá, we named

---

[9] For Teddy, a day without killing something was a day without sunshine.

the place the Republic of Panama and broke out our shovels. The Colombians were sore as a boil, but it's not as if they'd been serious people, like Europeans.[10]

Teddy was as fond of nature as cannibals are of missionary, and he didn't just stand there gawking at it, either. He did something about it, and charged right in and shot it between the eyes and had it stuffed and mounted. When Gifford Pinchot, a man who knew a few things about trees, told him the lumber companies were chopping them down left and right, Teddy was upset.[11] He and Pinchot decided to tell the lumber companies to go easy, and only cut down large or valuable trees and leave some of the rest. They called this "Conservation," and the word caught on. Teddy put 194 million acres in the National Park system, and called a Conservation Conference in Washington, where people got up and talked about preserving our natural resources so we could go on making money out of them for years. Pinchot said this was "a turning point in human history."[12]

During his second term Teddy became seriously involved in reforming English spelling to make it simpler and straightening out the European countries. He won a Nobel prize for helping with the Russo-Japanese peace negotiations.[13] He tried to get Germany, France, England, etc., to stop sharpening their swords and glaring at each other, which was quite futile and always had been, but at least he tried. Highly

---

[10] Teddy said, "You could no more make a deal with the Colombian rulers than you could nail currant jelly to the wall."

[11] He was afraid the outdoors would disappear and he'd be reduced to popping at squirrels in the Rose Garden.

[12] Well, it seemed like it at the time.

[13] When someone suggested he follow this up with a worldwide disarmament conference, he was *horrified*. He loved a good war. It was bad, or other people's, wars he didn't like.

civilized places that had always considered us a bunch of hooligans in coonskin caps began to eye us with new respect.[14]

Nothing came of the spelling reform, however.

When his term was up he appointed Taft to be the next President and said he was going to retire quietly and invisibly to shoot things in Africa, with plenty of reporters and a full film crew to make a movie about him and a magazine contract to write about it.

He said, "No President has ever enjoyed himself as much as I."

Strange as it may seem, even back in those golden days typesetters weren't infallible. After McKinley's assassination the newspapers covered Teddy's swearing-in, and in his haste somebody reached for a "b" instead of an "o." Next morning New Yorkers read that "for sheer democratic dignity, nothing could exceed the moment when, surrounded by the Cabinet and a few distinguished citizens, Mr. Roosevelt took his simple bath, as President of the United States."

The story was picked up abroad, so that the English too could read about this quaint but oddly moving American ritual.

---

[14] Maybe they admired the way we got our hands on Panama. It *was* pretty slick.

William Howard Taft

1909–1913

★

William Howard Taft was the world's largest President. He was bigger than Grover Cleveland I and II put together,[1] and when he sat down at his desk he could hardly reach it. After he squeezed into the White House they had to build him a special bathtub, and large groups of people had their picture taken lounging around in it together.

A newspaper reporter said he looked "like an American bison—a gentle, kind one." Indeed, there's a photograph of him, taken when he was governor of the Philippines, sitting on a water buffalo. He is correctly dressed as befits a governor and wears a Panama hat and carries a riding crop, and the line of spreading mass from the crown of his hat to the feet of the buffalo is artistically very satisfying. He doesn't look as if this was a joke, or a photo opportunity. He looks like a man about to go somewhere on a water buffalo.[2]

Plenty of candidates go all coy and say they don't really care about being President one way or the other, and they can take it or leave it, but Taft *really* didn't want to be President. He said politics made him sick. He said all his life all he wanted was to be a Supreme Court justice. His wife Nellie had other plans. When she was an impressionable young thing of seventeen she'd spent a week in the White House as a guest of the Hayeses, and she loved every minute of it. Then and there she vowed she'd only marry a man who could be President and take her back to her dream house. Compared to being First Lady, she thought judicial life would be pretty tame,[3] and she led him down Pennsylvania Avenue like an ox to the slaughter.

---

[1] You can't confuse him with Cleveland—Cleveland looked like a walrus. Taft looked like a buffalo, which is quite a different animal.

[2] What did you expect, roller skates?

[3] "An awful groove," she called it, which was slang for pretty tame.

Taft had been Teddy Roosevelt's Secretary of War after he got back from the Philippines, and Teddy said sure, he could be on the Supreme Court if he wanted to, but Nellie jumped in a cab and ran round to the White House for a private chat. She told Teddy how much nicer it would be if Taft could be President instead.[4] So Teddy said okay, and Taft was President.[5] The *Washington Post* congratulated Nellie rather pointedly.

There was a terrific blizzard the night before the inauguration, and Taft looked out the window and said, "Even the elements do protest." He was hoping it would snow so hard the whole thing would be called off permanently, but the elements had better sense than to mess with Nellie and it stopped.

Taft hated being President so much that he fell asleep whenever he wasn't playing golf. Nellie sat next to him at important conferences and poked him in the ribs to wake him up from time to time. Sometimes she answered questions for him, because she knew what he would have said if he'd stayed awake for the questions.

Unfortunately Nellie had a stroke early on, and while she was off the job his mind wandered more and more. Senator Dolliver said he was an amiable man surrounded by men who knew exactly what they wanted. What they wanted was land, and timber, and oil, and coal. While Taft was napping, his Secretary of the Interior tried to give Alaska to a pal of his, who thought it would be a good place to dig up some coal. Teddy Roosevelt's old forestry friend, Pinchot, squealed like a stuck pig and kicked up such a row about it that Taft had to fire him from the Forest Service. Well,

---

[4] Somehow Teddy misunderstood—no one knows why—and thought Taft *wanted* to be President.

[5] William Jennings Bryan lost, but he was used to it by this time and just shrugged.

people thought that wasn't what Teddy would have done. They thought maybe Taft was a friend of malefactors and a foe of trees.[6] They were disappointed in him.

When Nellie got better she took over her duties again and bought a cow to graze on the White House lawn and bring fresh milk to the kitchen. (Some say the cow was named Pauline Wayne, and some say Mooly-Wooly. My personal feeling is that Pauline Wayne was her formal, or registered, name, and Mooly-Wooly is what Nellie called her in moments of uncontrollable affection.) Then she sent for three thousand cherry trees from Japan, but they all had hoof-and-mouth disease and had to be burned, so she sent for three thousand more, and planted them in strategic spots to cause April traffic jams for generations yet unborn.

This was all very well, but it didn't solve the unions and Socialists and the painful misunderstandings between workers and their rightful employers that were still cropping up. Socialism was all the whirl, and people like Mabel Dodge gave terrific parties in honor of it, where everyone made passionate speeches about the workers and then passed the peyote and turned into Egyptian mummies, forest birds, etc.

Taft simply didn't know what to make of it.

He tried being the first President to throw out the opening ball of the baseball season, and Walter Johnson was so inspired that he pitched a one-hitter for the Senators against the Philadelphia Athletics for a final score of 3–0, but even that didn't help.

The truth is that people had been tired of the Tafts since almost before they'd unpacked. The only reason they bought newspapers now was to find out what Teddy was doing in Africa.

Teddy was doing plenty. Hardly anything taller than a box turtle was left standing. Skeptics wondered how he could shoot so many animals with the terrible eyes he had on him,

---

[6] He wasn't. He was just sleepy.

and it was quietly explained that when he pointed his gun at a lion, various other people pointed their guns too, just in case. One way or another, that lion was in trouble.[7] From time to time he left the hired help behind to stuff elephants and went on triumphal tours around Europe. The citizens lined the streets and cheered themselves hoarse as if Teddy were President of the world.[8]

Back home, people were looking forward to the next election.

For the Democrats there was a liberal sort of fellow named Bob La Follette who'd been doing liberal things in Wisconsin, but he drank too much brandy the night of the Periodical Publishers dinner and got wound up and spoke all night long, and people lost interest in him shortly before the sun came up. At the same dinner, a horse-faced intellectual named Woodrow Wilson, who used to be president of Princeton, spoke so briefly that everyone liked him better.[9]

Then Teddy came back from Africa with a whole pile of dead lions and lots of exhausted reporters. He'd changed his mind about Taft. He said that Taft "meant well, but he meant well feebly."[10] So the Republican party split, with the Conservatives saying they'd sooner vote for the dead lions than for Teddy, and the Progressives saying they'd vote for *anything* rather than Taft. Teddy called the Progressives the Bull Moose Party, because that was what he said he felt like, and rushed around campaigning. In Milwaukee somebody shot him but he paid no attention and went on with the speech, bleeding all down his front.[11]

---

[7] Ernest Hemingway was around twenty years old at the time—an impressionable age.

[8] Naturally Nellie Taft was very happy for him.

[9] People really hate listening to speeches after dinner. Why doesn't anyone realize this?

[10] By Teddy, "feebly" was a four-letter word.

[11] Running against Teddy could break your heart. Try to imagine it.

Taft wasn't very good at campaigning. When some reporters asked him what could be done about unemployment he said, "God knows."

The conservative Republicans voted for him anyway, and the progressive Republicans voted for Teddy, and everyone else voted for Wilson.

So Teddy packed up his reporters and went off to kill whatever it is people kill in Brazil, and in 1921 Harding made Taft Chief Justice of the Supreme Court. He was very good at it and very, very happy. He said, "The truth is that in my present life I don't remember that I ever was President."[12] He even got salty with Nellie and gave all her Faith Baldwin novels away to the Salvation Army.

Then she went upstairs and threw all his law books out the window.

Later, during rush hour, the magnificent chief-judicial rear loomed over New Hampshire Avenue as Taft rummaged in the hemlock hedge dragging out damp copies of the *Supreme Court Reporter*. Playing with Nellie, you never got to keep all the marbles.

---

[12] By this time lots of people didn't.

Woodrow Wilson

1913–1921

★

oodrow Wilson was very good and pure, and thought that everyone else could be good and pure too if they'd only follow his Fourteen-Point plan for a perfect world.[1] That way there'd never be any more wars, and all the countries would bring their little troubles to his League of Nations and live happily ever after.

Historians say he was a great genius because nobody had ever thought of the League of Nations before, but this is probably not true. It's the kind of thing small children think up all the time, and their parents tell them to hush.

Wilson was so right about everything that he never had to ask anyone's advice, because it couldn't possibly have been as right as his own. He only talked things over with his wives. *They* thought all his policies were simply lovely.

He was just crazy about his first wife, and when she died he went quite distracted and sat by her body for days, wringing his hands. Friends feared for his reason, so they introduced him to Edith Galt, and right away he was just crazy about her too, and married her almost immediately. He really needed a wife. You can't imagine how inconvenient it is to keep asking the presidential aides to stroke your brow when you've gone to bed with a headache, or to join you for your crackers and milk.[2]

As a general rule, Wilson much preferred women to men, and all his best friends were women. They were so much more admiring and sympathetic than men, and never argued or interrupted.[3]

Wilson had been a professor, and president of Princeton, and governor of New Jersey, and was widely respected for

---

[1] This established a commanding four-point lead over Moses, who gave up in despair.

[2] He drank a lot of milk. This is often a bad sign.

[3] He liked it that they couldn't vote, too. Voting would have spoiled their charm.

being an intellectual and very, very serious. He was serious because he had two rotten teeth right smack in the middle of where his smile would have been if he'd smiled. In private, though, with plenty of admiring women around, he unbent and recited funny limericks and did impersonations and, I'm told, often cranked up the phonograph and danced a merry jig. (This is not a thought you want to dwell on too much.) He also liked to read aloud to people and tell dialect stories in Cabinet meetings.[4]

William Allen White said shaking hands with Wilson was like shaking a "ten-cent pickled mackerel wrapped in brown paper."

The second wife, Edith, was one tough cookie. She'd only been to school for two years and didn't know beans about affairs of state, but Wilson didn't care. He discussed them with her anyway. He ignored his advisors entirely and stopped even saying "good morning" to his Cabinet, and he and Edith held policy meetings over many a glass of milk.[5]

He got elected the first time because of Teddy Roosevelt and his Bull Mooses[6] and the second time because he'd kept us out of the war in Europe. Then he decided we should go to war anyway. He cried *buckets* about it, but what could we do? Who else could show the Europeans how to be good and pure and follow the Fourteen Points?

Europe had been getting pretty tired of the war and thinking they might even call it off, but as soon as we got there it perked up again.

I don't recommend your trying to understand World War

---

[4] Professors and dentists get like that. They think people listen to them because they *want* to listen to them.

[5] She didn't like his advisors, or his Cabinet either, and never gave official dinners. She thought it was much nicer when it was just the two of them.

[6] Or because of Taft, depending on your point of view.

I unless you plan to make a career of it, and I don't recommend that either. As we all know, it consisted of opposing teams facing each other from trenches, waiting for someone to poke his head up and get shot. From time to time, small flimsy-looking planes chased each other around in the sky until one of them went down in flames. This was fun to watch but had no effect on the war. Mostly it was trenches. I don't know whose idea they were to start with, but four years later, when the war was over, the trenches were pretty much where they were in the beginning. There were more of them, because whenever things went badly the generals ordered everyone to fall out and dig more trenches, but geographically they hadn't moved much. Nobody complained. Nobody wanted to be the killjoy who said, "Hey, you know this trench idea? What if we tried something else for a change?" After all, the trenches were there, and digging them had been hard work, and they couldn't just walk off and leave them for someone to break a leg.[7]

Edith Wilson buckled right down to the war effort and bought a flock of sheep to graze on the White House lawn.[8] When she had them sheared their wool fetched a thousand dollars a pound at auction, because they were the White House sheep, and famous. She gave the money to the Red Cross. She felt it was the least she could do. Sometimes she even sewed pajamas for the Red Cross, and it was just delighted.

Finally the war was over and everyone came down with flu. It was a lot worse than the trenches.

Wilson and Edith went to the Versailles Peace Confer-

---

[7] In the next war we had foxholes instead, which were like trenches only shorter. They didn't work very well either. If you scrunched down people couldn't shoot at you, but they could drop or throw things at you. I don't know what the answer is.

[8] I can't find out what happened to Nellie Taft's cow.

ence in person, to be sure the other winners were kind and generous and didn't miss any Points. A reporter said Wilson was "like a virgin in a brothel, calling sturdily for a glass of lemonade." The Europeans liked his League of Nations scheme but they didn't think much of the other Points, especially the smarmy "Peace Without Vengeance" part. They told each other Wilson was a class-A ninny and gave Germany the complete rack-and-thumbscrews, bread-and-water treatment.

Wilson felt just awful about it. He was a wreck, but then, he'd always been a wreck. He had such terrible nervous indigestion that he'd bought his own stomach pump and carried it with him wherever he went.[9]

As soon as he got back from Versailles he went on a tour to preach about the League of Nations all over the country, but people didn't want to hear about it. They wanted to know what he was going to do about inflation and unemployment. He went right on talking about the League of Nations. He had a one-track mind.

Then he had a stroke, and came back to the White House and Edith put him in the bedroom and slammed the door. She stood outside it to make sure nobody talked to him. She didn't want anyone asking him hard questions, or finding out how sick he was. She just stood there for months, shaking her head "no."[10]

People worried. They thought maybe he was dead in there, or permanently unconscious, or a raving, drooling loony. Suddenly passersby noticed the bars on the White House windows. They'd been put there to keep Teddy's kids from throwing each other through the glass, but now they started to look kind of sinister. You can see how they would.

Wilson did sign some official papers, or at least Edith took

---

[9] Everyone's favorite dinner guest.
[10] She was directly descended from Pocahontas.

some papers into the bedroom and brought them back signed, and who am I to raise an eyebrow? Eyebrows were raised, certainly, but they weren't mine. She transferred the Secretary of Agriculture to Treasury, and when the Secretary of Interior quit she picked out a new one. She said it was what her husband would have wanted.

After four or five months of this, Secretary of State Lansing suggested that Wilson might turn over his duties to the Vice-President, and the next day he was reading the help-wanteds.[11] Well, it wasn't much of a suggestion. The Vice-President was that fellow Thomas Marshall who said, "What this country needs is a good five-cent cigar," and meant every word of it. When people asked him about taking over the presidency, he cried, "I can't even think about it!" When they tried to get him to do some work, he said he wasn't being paid to be President, and went out and played golf.

The *London Daily Mail* wrote, "Although Washington tongues are wagging vigorously no suggestion is heard that Mrs. Wilson is not proving a capable 'President.'" Others referred to the Petticoat Government, the Regency, and the Presidentress. Edith just folded her arms and stood there.

The Senate wouldn't ratify the Treaty of Versailles, so we could join Wilson's League of Nations, unless he made some changes. Edith went and asked him, and came back and said no, he wouldn't make any changes, so the Senate didn't, and we didn't.[12]

By spring he could limp around and talk a little, though he didn't make much sense, and Edith let him out from time to time. His grasp on reality hadn't improved, and he really thought the Democrats were going to nominate him for a

---

[11] Edith never could stand him.

[12] Maybe the League would have made out better if we'd joined, but I don't know. We joined the United Nations, didn't we?

third term. There wasn't enough left of him to nominate. Instead they picked a man named Cox, who was never heard from again, and a man named Frank Roosevelt, who was.

Wilson quite forgot himself and used words that even Edith hadn't known he knew.

Teddy Roosevelt said Wilson was "an utterly selfish and cold-blooded politician always," but Wilson didn't think he was selfish. He said he'd been sent here to carry out the teachings of Jesus Christ. He didn't say Who sent him, but we can guess.

Warren G. Harding

1921–1923

★

Mostly the democratic process works about as well as could be expected, but every so often it stirs up something from the bottom of the pond, and everyone goes "Yecch! What *is* it?" and then acts all injured innocence, as if they'd never marked a ballot in all their born days. Some of these unidentifiable objects were originally Vice-Presidents, so the public's not really to blame, but Harding was elected on his own with what the *New York Times* called "gigantic majorities . . . unprecedented in American politics."[1]

Harding owed everything to his wife and friends. He started out trying to teach in a one-room schoolhouse, which he said was the hardest job he ever had, and only lasted one term. Then he tried selling insurance, and then he wrote for the Marion, Ohio, *Democratic Mirror* for a while before they fired him.[2] Then he bought the bankrupt *Marion Star* and tried running that, and married Florence. Florence was five years older than he was and had an idea or two of her own.[3]

He was handsome and affable and friendly, and he happened to catch the eye of a man named Harry Daugherty. Daugherty owned Ohio and carried it around in his pocket. He had a lot of interesting connections, like Standard Oil, and a lot of dear friends known as The Ohio Gang to take care of. He needed a President of his very own, and when he saw Harding he said to himself, "Jeez, put some proper clothes on this hick and get him a decent haircut, he'd look *exactly* like a President." So he and Florence got together and sent Harding to Washington to start off as a senator.

Well, he just loved it. It was the very thing. He missed

---

[1] It was the first election women voted in. They needed more practice.

[2] The poet e.e. cummings said Harding was "the only man, woman or child / to write a simple declarative sentence / with seven grammatical errors."

[3] He called her the Duchess.

half the roll calls and had affairs with pretty ladies and enjoyed himself enormously, so when Daugherty came and suggested he move on to bigger and better things, Harding said no, he didn't want to be President, he just wanted to stay in the Senate and play. Then Daugherty went to Florence, and Florence went to work.[4] Nobody knows what she did to him, but pretty soon there was Harding wandering around in the original smoke-filled room, slightly drunk and looking bewildered.[5]

The nomination startled some people. It startled the *New York Times,* which called Harding's Senate record "faint and colorless" and added snidely, "We must go back to Franklin Pierce if we would seek a President who measures down to his political stature."

Harding campaigned by telling everyone that they could quit thinking about foreigners and all their foreign problems and get back to normalcy. There's no such word, but people knew what he meant and voted for him in droves.

On election day, I'm told that Florence said, "Well, Warren Harding, I have got you the presidency; what are you going to do with it?" and Harding said, "May God help me, for I need it." (No, I haven't the faintest idea how we know this. Were they bellowing at each other across the Mall? Was the bedroom bugged?)

Anyway, Florence was pleased as punch.[6] On inauguration day she threw open the gates and invited everyone in, and sightseers swarmed all over ripping souvenirs off the trees and bushes.[7] She loved being First Lady. Once she shook 6,756 hands in a single afternoon. She tried to keep a close eye on her husband so he wouldn't do anything he'd

---

[4] A fortune-teller had told her he was going to be President. She was just giving Destiny a hand.

[5] His father once said to him, "If you were a girl, Warren, you'd be in the family way all the time. You can't say No."

[6] So was Daugherty.

[7] I can't find out what happened to Edith Wilson's sheep.

regret, or say something dumb. She even rewrote his speeches for him, and he read them without noticing the difference.[8]

She was learning fast. Harding wasn't. He really did look like a President, but deep down he was shallow. He said to his secretary, "Jud, you have a college education, haven't you? I don't know what to do or where to turn. . . . Somewhere there must be a book that tells all about it. . . . But I don't know where that book is, and maybe I couldn't read it if I found it! . . . My God, but this is a hell of a place for a man like me to be in!"

When it all got too much for him, he'd go to the little green house on K Street and hang out with Daugherty's Ohio Gang. He wasn't always sure what they were up to, but he did know they were his buddies, and it made him feel warm all over to have his buddies around. Sometimes he played poker with them all night, trying to forget. He said, "Oftentimes . . . I don't seem to grasp that I am President." Then his buddies, who did grasp it, would give him a big hug and let him win the pot. They didn't mind when he picked his teeth after meals or chewed tobacco, or when he ran out of chewing tobacco and slit open a cigarette and chewed the insides instead.

Sometimes the Gang dropped by the White House, and Florence served the drinks upstairs in the private quarters. There wasn't any wine on the dinner table because of Prohibition, but you couldn't exactly entertain The Ohio Gang on decaf.

She liked to have him home where she could keep an eye on him, but occasionally he slipped out anyway.[9] Often she

---

[8] Some of them were hard to understand, but that wasn't Florence's fault. He never was quite sure what he was talking about.

[9] A certain Nan Britton claimed he was the father of her daughter, but the jury didn't see it her way.

didn't quite know where he was, which was most provoking.

He should have stuck with the women and stayed away from the poker players, who kept asking him for this and that. He was always happy to help out, because basically he was an amiable, kind-hearted fellow and fond of children and dogs and his buddies. He should never have made Charley Forbes head of the Veterans Administration, because Charley stole the veterans' money and went to prison, but how was Harding to know?[10]

The Teapot Dome was another mistake. The Teapot Dome was a whole lot of oil underneath Wyoming, and it was supposed to be federal oil, waiting there until the navy needed it. Harding had made his friend Albert Fall Secretary of Interior, and when Fall said he was the very man to watch over this oil, Harding told him to go ahead and watch over it. No one was more surprised than Harding when Fall turned around and sold the stuff.

Accidents like that kept happening. It's really depressing when so many of your friends start committing suicide and going to jail that you can hardly scratch up a decent poker game, so he and Florence decided to take a nice long train trip across the country, all the way to Alaska, which is about as far as it goes. They figured if they smiled and waved a lot along the way, people wouldn't notice the string of scandals crackling and sputtering back home. Harding kept walking up and down the train asking reporters and the hired help what *they'd* do if *their* friends turned out to be a bunch of bums.

Along about Seattle he was a bit under the weather, so they detoured to San Francisco to rest. By August second he was feeling ever so much better, and Florence was reading aloud to him in his room, and he just sort of died.

---

[10] What Florence knew and when she knew it is something else again. She was no honor student, but she wasn't half as dumb as he was.

There is not a shred of evidence that she poisoned him, and I don't see how you can be so mean. Five days later, when she got off the train in Washington, anyone could see she was *not* carrying a half-empty bottle of prussic acid. It's true that she wouldn't let them do an autopsy, but plenty of people think autopsies are nasty, even people who've hardly poisoned anyone at all. And yes, she was cool as a cucumber at the funeral, but maybe she was all torn up inside. And she was overheard talking to his body in the coffin, saying, "No one can hurt you now, Warren," but surely there's nothing sinister in *that*? Yes, maybe he would have been impeached if he'd come home alive, but then again, maybe he wouldn't have been.[11] And yes, she did grab up and burn all his papers and letters, but she was just tidying up. She wouldn't have wanted the Coolidges peeking at them. If there was one thing Florence hated—and there was—it was Coolidges.

Besides, everyone agrees Harding died of a stroke, or pneumonia, or apoplexy, or a blood clot, or food poisoning, or something.

Florence gave his dog, Laddie Boy,[12] to the servants and washed her hands of the whole business, but the scandals kept right on popping up like toadstools all over town. It got so the Harding administration was what people meant when they said "corruption" or "sleaze" or "ugh."

Harding said, "I am not fit for this office and never should have been here." Teddy Roosevelt's daughter Alice said, "Harding was not a bad man. He was just a slob."

Florence didn't say anything.

---

[11] And maybe I'm the real Anastasia Romanov.
[12] Some authorities will tell you Laddie Boy was a Scottie; others, a Collie. In his pictures he looks a lot more like an Airedale. I had a dog like that once myself.

Calvin Coolidge

1923–1929

★

Calvin Coolidge was born in Vermont and weaned on a pickle.[1] He never said much of anything to anyone, so that when he did say something, like "The business of America is business," it sounded deep, or anyway a lot deeper than if he'd always been nattering away about this and that, and people wrote long articles considering what it meant.

Many people felt he could hardly be worse than Harding, but there were dissenting opinions. Oswald Harrison Villard of the *New York Evening Post* wrote, "And now the Presidency sinks low indeed. I doubt if it has ever fallen into the hands of a man so cold, so narrow, so reactionary, so uninspiring, so unenlightened, or who has done less to earn it than Calvin Coolidge."

When Harding died Coolidge was visiting his father on his farm in Vermont. His father was a notary public, and he found the presidential oath of office in some book he had lying around and swore Cal in by the light of a kerosene lamp at a quarter of three in the morning in the family dining room. Then Cal went back to bed, as he was always a firm believer in getting plenty of sleep.

This was completely illegal, of course, since a notary in Vermont can only swear in people who plan to be working in Vermont, but for a public relations move you just couldn't beat it, especially the kerosene lamp.

Cal believed in living simply and not throwing good money away. In the White House he prowled around in his nightshirt with his skinny bare legs sticking out and kept checking the pantry to make sure nobody was buying extra food. The chef said he couldn't cook without groceries, and quit.

Before and after his Washington career the Coolidges

---

[1] That's what Alice Roosevelt Longworth said, but she may have been guessing.

lived in half a rented double house in Northampton, Massachusetts, and Grace made do.[2]

Grace was a perfectly charming lady with a pet raccoon named Rebecca that she carried around with her. Nobody could figure out why she married him. *He* said it was because he "outsat everyone else," but marrying Silent Cal just because he wouldn't get out of your living room seems like an extreme solution.

Grace really loved life in Washington because sometimes she was allowed to have visitors or go to dinner parties, and chat with people.[3] Mostly she had her husband with her, but people hardly noticed. He just stared at his plate, and sometimes at his watch. His idea of entertainment was to make selected congressmen eat breakfast with him at eight-thirty in the morning, an hour when many selected congressmen aren't at their sharpest. The recipe he gave the kitchen for breakfast cereal was four pecks of whole wheat mixed with one peck of whole rye, boiled until it was soft enough to chew.[4]

At one of the congressional breakfasts everyone watched while Cal poured some coffee into his saucer and added a splash of milk. Several guests respectfully did the same, and then Cal put the saucer down on the floor for his dog. The others didn't know what to do with theirs, but they didn't mind because it gave them a Coolidge story to tell. (It might have been his idea of a joke. Sometimes it was hard to know.)

---

[2] It was wonderful what she could whip up with a little salted water and an onion.

[3] Cal didn't let her visit with anyone important, like Cabinet wives, because he didn't think she was all that bright, but he couldn't keep her locked up *entirely*.

[4] This was very wholesome and modern and just what we now know we should eat, but folks back then were so ignorant they thought it was horse feed.

Queen Marie of Romania came for a state visit. She was a famous party person and just loved going to visit people, but Cal only let her stay for an hour and forty-five minutes, including all those ceremonial greetings, and dinner and dessert and coffee, and then finding everyone's coats, and the ceremonial farewells. This may have been a world record.

You might think Calvin Coolidge wasn't a playful President, but you'd be dead wrong. He had his fun-loving side, and liked to push all the buttons on his desk at once and watch his aides come running. Once, on a fishing trip, he made his Secret Service agent put the worm on the hook for him, and just at the right moment he gave the line a quick jerk and impaled the man's thumb. And there was an alarm bell in the White House he could ring whenever he wanted to peek through the curtains and watch the guards and policemen go bananas.

He had his little sensual self-indulgences, too, and loved to eat his boiled wheat-and-rye in bed while people rubbed Vaseline into his hair. He had that very thin, fine, reddish hair, and his forehead was slowly getting bigger and bigger. This may have been his main concern while in office. There was a portrait of John Adams in the Red Room that he hated to look at because John was pretty bald. He couldn't help seeing it from his chair at the dinner table, and it bothered him more and more until finally he got Ike Hoover, the chief usher, to smear turpentine on Adams's shiny scalp until it looked hairy, and then he liked it much better.

In the summer of '24 Calvin, Jr., who was sixteen, got a blister on his toe playing lawn tennis and died of blood poisoning. Coolidge was said to be dreadfully upset about this, though it was hard to tell when he was dreadfully upset and when he wasn't.[5]

He ran for reelection, if "ran" isn't too strong a word, on

---

[5] George Creel said he was "distinguishable from the furniture only when he moved."

the slogan "Keep Cool and Keep Coolidge," which the public correctly understood was not a cigarette ad but meant
that the whole country was rich and happy and having a
wonderful time and it was all because of Cal. Naturally they
voted for him instead of the Democrat John Davis or the
Progressive Bob La Follette, who were trying to tell them
that everyone *wasn't* rich and happy.[6]

Coolidge believed that business and Wall Street knew
what was best for themselves, and as long as everyone was
happy, why bother them? William Allen White called him "an
economic fatalist with a God-given inertia. He knew nothing
and refused to learn." (There's one in every crowd.) Will
Rogers asked him how he stayed so healthy, when being
President had gotten Wilson so wrought up it made him ill,
and Coolidge said, "By avoiding the big problems."[7]

Folks thought he must be working hard because they
never saw him out doing anything else, like pitching
horseshoes, but he wasn't. One of his Secret Service
agents—not the one with the fishhook in his thumb—felt
Coolidge should have some sort of hobby or interest in life,
or at least get some exercise, so an electric horse was
installed in one of the bedrooms. Sometimes Coolidge got
on it and it bounced him around. Sometimes he let the
Secret Service agent take turns with him. It was fun, sort
of.

People have the feeling that nothing much happened during the Coolidge administration, but it only seemed that way.
Leopold and Loeb kidnapped and killed little Bobby Franks.
A tornado redistributed much of Illinois. Ma Ferguson was
elected governor of Texas. Bootleggers bootlegged. King
Tut's tomb was opened. Ford threw caution to the winds
and started painting cars green and maroon as well as black.

---

[6] This is not a good thing to try to tell people. They don't
want to hear about it.

[7] He took long naps too.

John Scopes was convicted of teaching evolution. Gertrude Ederle swam the English Channel and Lindbergh flew to Paris. *The Jazz Singer* was released. Sacco and Vanzetti were executed. Ten people died of heart attacks while listening to the Dempsey-Tunney fight on the radio, Babe Ruth kept hitting home runs, and *Show Boat* opened. Al Capone went to jail and the first Mickey Mouse cartoon appeared. The Valentine's Day massacre took out fourteen of Bugs Moran's boys. Everyone sang "Ain't We Got Fun" and pretended to be Scott and Zelda.[8]

In August, 1927, Coolidge was in Rapid City, South Dakota, which was his idea of a place to go on vacation, and called a press conference in the local high school. The reporters, who were quite unhinged already from hanging around Rapid City watching the dust blow back and forth and waiting for something to happen, all filed past him in a long line and he handed each one a folded slip of paper like a fortune-cookie fortune. Each piece of paper said, "I do not choose to run for President in nineteen twenty-eight." He spelled out the year so that the message came to twelve words.[9] The *New York Times* reporter said, "It is believed here that the President will say nothing more," and he never did, so everyone buckled down to figure out what he meant by it. They asked his wife and all his aides and advisors, but they didn't know either. Analysts thought the word "choose" was peculiar, and "run" was open to question too. One group felt he wanted to be drafted, and another that he wouldn't mind *being* President as long as he didn't have to *run.*

In the end, it turned out he just meant "no."

When they asked him to sum up his administration in a

---

[8] Everyone except the Coolidges, that is.
[9] People were always tallying up Coolidge's words like that. Mostly they could use their fingers.

farewell speech, he said, "Goodbye, I have had a very enjoyable time in Washington."

It wasn't exactly a memorable presidency, but what happened next was so much worse that everyone looked back wistfully on those happy golden years when whatsisname was in the White House.

When he died in 1933, Dorothy Parker said, "How can they tell?"

Herbert Hoover

1929–1933

★

erbert Hoover led a very exciting life, but the excitement kind of rolled off of him so that he stayed boring underneath. He even looked boring. He had a pudgy baby-face and parted his hair in the middle, and there are no pictures of him smiling. He didn't see what there was to smile about.[1] He was a Quaker and always worked hard, and crossed his t's and dotted his i's.

With even the most ordinary luck he might have made a perfectly acceptable President. Is it his fault that "Hoover-ville" means a town built out of flattened paint cans and "Hoover blankets" are newspapers under your clothes? This is not a nice way to go down in history, and it's a shame, that's what it is.

Hoover was orphaned at the age of nine, and schoolchildren were told that he picked potato bugs off the potato plants for a penny a hundred. He did, but he wasn't buying day-old bread with the pennies as the schoolchildren were allowed to assume. He was saving up to buy fireworks. Later he studied mining and managed gold mines in Australia and married Lou and went to China as chief engineer of the Chinese Imperial Bureau of Mines. Lou learned Chinese and became an expert on Chinese vases.[2] After that they lived in England, Australia, New Zealand, Burma, and Russia. When they found a book about mines called *De Re Metallica,* written in 1556 by Georgius Agricola, they spent five years translating it from Latin into English. They thought it would be more interesting in English, but it wasn't.

---

[1] Wilson wouldn't smile either, but on him it looked intellectual. On Hoover it just looked cross.

[2] The Chinese are famous for vases, available in an assortment of styles, called Dynasties. Nobody knows what they wanted with so many vases. They didn't know themselves, but every time a new Dynasty came along they figured this would be the one that made it all worthwhile, and fired up the kiln again. There were vases *everywhere.* Their wives were furious.

During the Boxer Rebellion in China Hoover had been in charge of distributing food, and he found this so exhilarating that he went on distributing food all over the world during and after World War I. Everywhere you looked, there was Hoover holding out a can of beans. Pretty soon he was a household word for food, mines, and traveling, so Harding and Coolidge made him Secretary of Commerce.[3]

He ran for President by telling people the country was still so rich and happy that "the slogan of progress is changing from the full dinner pail to the full garage." The Democrat, Al "The Happy Warrior" Smith, was a Catholic, and got left in a crumpled heap gasping in the dust by the roadside.[4] At his inauguration Hoover said, "In no nation are the fruits of accomplishment so secure." Well, nobody's right *all* the time.

In October the stock market crashed, and everything else kind of caved in after it. This was called the Great Depression because it went on and *on,* unlike previous depressions, which had always stopped after a while.

There are many complex theories about the Depression, but Coolidge, who was writing a newspaper column at the time, put it most neatly. He wrote, "When more and more people are thrown out of work, unemployment results."

Hoover knew exactly what people should do when they were out of work and out of money. They should move in with their neighbors and relatives and open a line of credit at the grocery store. When all the neighbors and relatives ran out of money and the grocery store went out of business, then the cities and states should do something, even if *they* didn't have any money because nobody was paying taxes. They should hire people for civic construction proj-

---

[3] I *told* you he was boring.

[4] Even New York, where he'd been governor four times, wouldn't vote for him. *There's* gratitude for you.

ects, and to pick up newspapers and orange peels in the park. The federal government should stay clear out of it, though, because it was none of its business, and federal handouts lead to waste and corruption, and besides, the whole thing was only "a temporary halt in the prosperity of a great people."[5]

The Hoovers were known for giving nice parties for friends of theirs, who weren't a bit Depressed. They graciously paid for these themselves, and the guests all admired Lou's many Chinese vases and pretended they'd been crazy about *De Re Metallica* and couldn't put it down.

The Hoovers had a small dog named Piney, a large dog named Snowflake, and a German shepherd named Tut who hated Hoover and made no secret of the fact.

Lou was almost uncontrollably interested in the Girl Scouts, and filled the White House with little girls in green uniforms selling cookies. Herbert liked to fish.[6] When people kept badgering him to do something about the Great Depression, he said, "Prosperity cannot be restored by raids upon the public treasury," and went to his fishing camp on the Rapidan in the Blue Ridge mountains.[7]

Everyone who wasn't starving went around saying, "Well, it isn't as if anyone was actually *starving*." This wasn't strictly true. People were starving, but they were doing it so gradually they didn't get much publicity, and also coming down with the complaints you get from living on fried flour-and-water paste. People from the farms went to

---

[5] He could tell it was nothing serious because he still had four million preinflation dollars from his engineering company.

[6] In 1963 he wrote a book called *Fishing for Fun and To Wash Your Soul.* Don't miss it.

[7] Fishing is a good hobby for Presidents. It's peaceful and relaxing and gets the reporters and Secret Service agents all wet and muddy and lost.

the cities to look for work, and people from the cities went
to the farms to look for food, and other people went nowhere in particular, mostly by boxcar. Resourceful types
managed to get thrown in jail, where it was warmer, or set
fire to forests so they could hire on for three dollars a day
as emergency firefighters.

Hoover said in his memoirs that selling apples on street
corners had nothing to do with the Depression but was just
a fine business to be in. "Many persons left their jobs for
the more profitable one of selling apples," he explained.
This was foolish of them, since selling apples was a mug's
game compared to shining shoes. A shoe-shine kit cost less
than a box of apples and it was a permanent investment,
unlike apples, which go away after you've sold them. The
New York Times went outside to count the shoe-shiners on
one block of West Forty-third Street, and there were nineteen of them, ranging in age from sixteen to seventy. It was
the Golden Age of shiny shoes.

In the summer of 1932, some twenty thousand veterans
marched on Washington wanting their bonuses ahead of
time, and hung around ruining the grass and wouldn't leave
until Hoover sent General Douglas MacArthur with some
cavalry and infantry and some tanks and bayonets and tear
gas, and a box of matches for the tents. A couple of the
veterans accidentally got killed, and the rest realized they
were camping in the wrong place and left town. The *Times*
said "Few knew whither to go," but they went anyway.
Hoover said they probably weren't veterans at all, just Communists.

He tried to distract people by making "The Star-Spangled
Banner" our national anthem, but only the chosen few who
could reach that high note near the end were distracted. In
fact, folks were getting so undistractable that he was forced
to sign the Emergency Relief Act to lend the states $300
million for soup ingredients. This went against his deepest

convictions, but he needn't have worried, as the thing got so tangled in red tape that by the end of the year only $30 million had been lent.[8]

Hoover was rather strict with the White House staff and the servants had orders to stay out of sight. If he or Lou came into a room and there was a servant in it, that servant was supposed to jump into a closet and hide until the coast was clear. Sometimes there was no room for the coats and jackets because of all the servants crouching in there in the dark and mashing the galoshes.

Biographers try to explain Herbert Hoover by saying he was an orphan and couldn't help it. This is nonsense. Plenty of orphans grow up perfectly normal.

After Hoover stopped being President he went right on being Hoover for a long time, distributing cans of beans and serving on worthy committees and making speeches about how Roosevelt was wrecking everything. He gave all his government salaries away to charity, and after a while some people forgave him for the Great Depression. "A conscientious public servant," they called him, stifling a yawn.

Others always bore a grudge.

---

[8] When asked about it, federal officials smiled vaguely and changed the subject.

Franklin Delano Roosevelt

1933–1945

★

Roosevelt was President for so long that by the time he died everyone under twenty thought "President" was his first name, and couldn't figure out what we were going to call the new man.

Roosevelt was a gentleman from a family with money so old it didn't crackle any more, it whispered. The name was originally "van Roosevelt," so you can see the kind of thing. Nobody like this can be elected in a proper democracy unless they get cut down to size somehow, so the Great Campaign Manager up there gave him polio in 1921, when he was thirty-nine. His legs were crippled, so he had to scoot around in a wheelchair or clump along on eight-pound leg braces with a cane and someone to lean on. The historian Paul Conkin wrote, "Polio made the aristocratic Roosevelt into an underdog. For him it replaced the log cabin."

In a wheelchair Roosevelt didn't look half so tall and snooty, and besides, you're supposed to be nice to the crippled and admire their pluck.

You could hardly accuse him of fooling around with women, either. It would be morbid. The poor fellow couldn't even use his *legs,* for heaven's sake.

As far as we know, he didn't fool around with a *lot* of women.[1] First there was Lucy Mercer, his wife's secretary, and I've heard he thought about divorcing Eleanor and marrying her until his mother threatened to cut off his allowance and he changed his mind.[2] Then there was his own secretary, Missy LeHand, but that hardly counts because it lasted twenty years and heavens, they were just like some old

---

[1] I don't put much stock in those wartime tales about Princess Martha of Norway, do you?

[2] She just *never* liked his friends. She'd dragged him away on a cruise to take his mind off Eleanor, and was mad as a wet hen when it didn't work.

married couple and slept in adjoining bedrooms.[3] After Missy's death he took up with Lucy again, so you can see what a faithful fellow he really was. Lucy was with him at Warm Springs when he died, but she beetled off the premises before Eleanor and the press showed up.[4]

Anyway, we've had Presidents who couldn't be trusted alone with a lady *armadillo,* and I think we should change the subject.

At college Roosevelt was pretty extracurricular, and his GPA showed it, but he did write various stirring articles on football and school spirit for the *Harvard Crimson.* At Columbia Law he was bored to tears and flunked some subjects and dropped out, but he passed the New York bar exams anyway. Democratic leaders took an interest in him because his name sounded familiar[5] and he had enough money to run for the state senate from the wrong place. They talked him into being the Democratic candidate in Dutchess County, which was like running for Pope in Israel, but he rode around shaking hands in such a very bright red touring car that everyone noticed him and he won. Then in 1912 he said such nice things about Wilson that Wilson made him Assistant Secretary of the Navy, just like Teddy only without the Spanish-American War.[6] Then he got plowed under with Cox in the Harding election, and went on to be governor of

---

[3] This was all right with Eleanor. Eleanor had other things on her mind, but we needn't go into that. Anyway, she wasn't home much.

[4] His son Elliott wrote us a book about it all. Don't kids say the darnedest things?

[5] Teddy was only his fifth cousin, but he was Eleanor's uncle, and President when he gave her away at the wedding. All eyes were upon him, which was right where Teddy felt eyes belonged.

[6] Wilson called him a "handsome young giant." Well, now, *really.*

New York a couple of times, and by 1932 everyone knew his name even if they couldn't pronounce it.

When he got nominated for President, the *New York Times* ran a front-page box explaining about his name. They said it was Dutch and pronounced "Rose-velt," in two syllables, with a long "o." You'd think folks would have noticed before, since he'd been around all this time and his cousin was the most famous person in the world for years, but they hadn't, and they still didn't. Democrats called him "Rose-a-velt" and Republicans called him "Rooze-uh-veld," or sometimes "Rosenfeld," claiming it was his original name, which it wasn't.[7]

He campaigned against Hoover by saying he'd cut government spending and hand out lots of government money, which he seemed to think was no problem.[8] He said there was going to be a whole New Deal, and folks figured it couldn't be much worse than the Old Deal, even if he had filched the phrase from Mark Twain. His supporters kept singing "Happy Days Are Here Again," a ditty that subsequent candidates keep recycling with varying degrees of success. He buried Hoover 472-52.

There's nothing like a fresh President when you've been feeling down in the mouth, and here was this one in a long flowing cape like Superman, grinning like a horsecollar with a cigarette holder jammed in his teeth and that big booming laugh, and besides he's crippled, and you think *you've* got troubles? He told people that the only thing they had to fear was fear itself, which was an over-

---

[7] Strict conservatives never called him anything but "That Man," and ordered the servants to scissor any mention of him out of the morning papers before carrying them into the breakfast room with their tatters fluttering.

[8] He said, "If you have spent a year in bed trying to wiggle your big toe, then anything else seems easy."

statement and left out a few odds and ends but sounded great.

He'd promised action, and right away there was action. He was the one who started this "first hundred days" contest, where reporters keep asking new Presidents what *they've* done in *their* first hundred days, and plenty of them haven't even unpacked yet or figured out where the bathrooms are. Roosevelt closed the banks down for four days, to stop people from taking their money home to hide under the couch cushions, and repealed Prohibition, so he could mix his friends a nice martini in the Oval Study, and put a woman in the Cabinet as Secretary of Labor, and stirred up a whole snowstorm of legislation and federal agencies with letters instead of names, like the TVA and the NRA and the PWA and the RFC and the AAA and the CCC, so nobody knew what they were supposed to be doing. He set Brain Trusters to running back and forth in the hallways, and Eleanor running around everywhere else and reporting back to him.[9]

Soon people were swarming all over the country getting paid by the government for useful works, like building long stone walls along deserted stretches of highway, photographing sharecroppers, and planting endless rows of tree seedlings, some of which survived, on every hillside. Eleanor crawled through coal mines and came out very dirty saying the miners had a right to complain a lot, and organize and strike. There was always something going on, usually Eleanor, to read about in the papers, and you know how this cheers people up even while they're stirring the flour-and-water paste for lunch.

The conservatives grew quite hysterical and told each other the end of the world was at hand. Social Security had

---

[9] She logged forty thousand miles in the first year and that was just a warm-up. Her Secret Service code name was "Rover."

been the last straw.[10] In 1936 they ran Alf Landon, calling him "The Kansas Coolidge."[11] Their slogan was "Save America from Socialism," and their platform was all about how unconstitutional Roosevelt was, and how "even the integrity and authority of the Supreme Court have been flaunted."[12]

Landon carried Maine and Vermont, giving birth to the encouraging thought for future candidates, "As Maine goes, so goes Vermont."

By 1940 John Garner was tired of being Vice-President while Roosevelt got all the attention, and Roosevelt wanted the totally radical Henry Wallace instead. The convention wanted someone just the teensiest bit more politically normal, but Eleanor rushed unexpectedly to the podium and made a speech for Wallace that blew them away and he was in.[13]

The Republicans said that not only was Roosevelt still a socialist, he was helping Britain fight Hitler, and if we didn't watch it we'd be fighting Hitler too, and maybe Hitler wasn't the pleasantest fellow in the world, but at least he wasn't soft on Communism like some people they knew. Their candidate was Wendell Willkie, who'd been a Democrat all his life until he noticed the New Deal nibbling away at his business profits and saw the error of his ways.

Political verses and insults had been shrinking down to slogans, due to Ford's discovery of the automobile bumper,

---

[10] Germany had started it in the 1880s and England in 1911, so anyone could see it was un-American, and those people who still had jobs would probably quit them immediately and just sit around waiting to be sixty-five.

[11] Talk about charisma.

[12] If you've got 'em, flaunt 'em, *I* always say.

[13] People got so sick of Eleanor jokes and Eleanor cartoons that First Ladies ever since have kept their heads down and stuck to roadside daffodils, chamber music concerts, party dresses, and kindly causes.

and Willkie's slogan was "No Man is Good Three Times."[14] The Democrats replied, "Better a Third-Termer than a Third-Rater." Willkie carried some midwestern states.

This brings us to December 7, 1941, the "date which will live in infamy," though it seems too bad to blame it on the calendar when it was the Japanese that dropped the bombs. Roosevelt called a joint session of Congress, and Congress agreed to go to war, 82–0 in the Senate and 388–1 in the House.[15]

War turned out to be just what the doctor ordered to put a stop to the Depression, and everyone quit planting rows of little trees and rushed off to enlist and make tanks and guns and pay taxes again, and the economy was back in Biscuit City.

World Wars I and II should not be confused with each other even though many of the same players took part. The second one was easier to understand because it had Hitler, who invaded Poland and committed many Nazi atrocities too nasty to mention and wasn't a nice person at all. The first war had more trenches, but the second one had more bombs. Bombs were so much more interesting to photograph than trenches that the newsreel was born. It was a little like television news, only it was a week old and cost money to watch.

The people to remember from World War II are Hitler, Hirohito—or Tojo; you needn't remember both—Mussolini, Churchill, Stalin, De Gaulle, and Roosevelt, who was *still* President.[16]

---

[14] Well, that's what he said. I wouldn't know, myself. I lead a very quiet life.

[15] Miss Jeanette Rankin (R., Montana) hadn't changed her mind since she voted against the other war in 1917. All the other congresspersons hissed and booed, but she took no notice.

[16] Come to think of it, it wouldn't hurt to remember General Eisenhower too. You'll see why later.

There were machine guns on the White House roof and a bomb shelter in the basement and a gas mask dangling from the presidential wheelchair, but Roosevelt's black Scottie, Fala, who had grown quite portly bumming goodies from the staff, still went with him everywhere and his Fireside Chats still went out over the radio, mellow as ever. Eleanor was still busy. They called her "Public Energy Number One," and she was going through Secret Service agents the way you and I go through a box of Kleenex.

By 1944 everyone was so used to Roosevelt being President that they hardly noticed Thomas Dewey, the governor of New York, running against him by calling him an invalid and a Communist, which wasn't exactly new stuff, but they were all so busy down at Republican Headquarters they didn't have time to think of anything else. Besides, there was a war on, and it was going pretty well as wars go, so who needed a new President?

Vice-President Wallace was still totally radical, so Roosevelt agreed to tone things down a bit and substituted a Missouri senator named Harry S Truman. Nobody knew much about him, but it didn't matter as Roosevelt was clearly going to be President forever and ever.

Actually, he hadn't been feeling quite the thing lately, but he did want to stick it out and help fix the peace arrangements and make sure the colonial empires stopped being colonial empires and the United Nations happened. He thought he'd do better at all this than Wilson had, but he died on April 12, 1945.

Even his worst enemies were surprised. They'd thought he was permanent. He almost was.

Harry S. Truman

1945–1953

★

Harry S[1] Truman made such a change from Roosevelt that people were quite nervous. They said he was just a *little* man, and they remembered Roosevelt as being bigger.[2] Union leader Al Whitney called him a ribbon clerk. Everyone was afraid he wouldn't do any better as President than he had at other things he'd tried.

He was the son of a farmer who'd made quite a local reputation as a mule trader too, and he wanted to be a professional musician when he grew up. Nothing came of this plan. He had thick glasses and was no good at games. After high school he worked as a railroad timekeeper, mail room clerk, bank clerk, farmer, postmaster, and road overseer. Then he tried being a partner in a lead mine and an oil prospecting firm, but those didn't work out either.

By the time he was thirty-three he was still living at home and reading the help-wanteds, so he figured what the hell and enlisted in World War I. He was pretty good at that. The men called him "Captain Harry," and he learned some bad language and felt a lot taller and braver, but then the war was over and there he was back home in Missouri, playing Chopin till all hours of the night and reading the help-wanteds again. He went partners in a haberdashery shop in Kansas City, but he always wore such gaudy sport shirts and bow ties that people were embarrassed to shop there and it went bankrupt.

He'd tried everything but politics, so he had a go at that. He knew someone who knew Big Tom Pendergast, the Democratic boss of Kansas City, and pretty soon he was a Jackson County judge, not bad for a fellow who never went

---

[1] The S didn't stand for anything. It was his middle name. He was the only President in history whose middle name was S.

[2] Roosevelt was six foot two when he stood up and Truman was only five foot nine. He barely came up to De Gaulle's shoulder, even with a big hat on.

to college, but after the next election there was poor Harry on the street again, peddling memberships in the Kansas City Automobile Club. Then he went partners in a Missouri state bank and, well, I'll give you three guesses what happened to *that* bank. Finally Pendergast pulled some more strings[3] and Harry went off to the Senate—the *United States* Senate—and stayed ten years.

The Senate is set up so that it can't go bankrupt no matter who gets into it, and Missourians were greatly relieved that whatever Harry got mixed up in, it would be in Washington and not in Missouri, as long as they kept sending him back there. Little did they know.

In the White House the Trumans were so unpretentious it was practically pretentious of them, except for moving in with three pianos. Harry got up at five-thirty every morning and took a brisk walk. His wife, Bess, had once been a basketball star and famous for being able to whistle through her teeth, but those days were over. She wouldn't give interviews or press conferences, and when people did catch sight of her, her clothes were so unpretentious they felt she must have them specially made, since surely you couldn't buy things like that in a *shop*.

Their daughter, Margaret, played on all three pianos and sang. Sometimes she sang in public, which gave rise to the most famous incident of the whole administration, when the *Washington Post* music critic, Paul Hume, suggested she should take up some quite different and preferably silent hobby, and Harry wrote to him saying if he ever met Hume, then he, Hume, would "need a new nose and perhaps a supporter below." This was considered undignified and ar-

---

[3] No, this was *before* Pendergast went to jail for tax evasion and bribes.

tistically insensitive of him and besides, Hume's views were widely supported by other music critics.[4]

Truman had been Vice-President for only eighty-three days, and both times he'd met Roosevelt, Roosevelt forgot to tell him what was happening, or how the war was going, or anything useful like that, so when he found he was President it came as a shock.[5]

It was one of those busy seasons in the White House, too. In his first four months the war with Germany ended, and the atom bomb got dropped, and the war with Japan ended, and the United Nations geared up. It was a zoo. Harry put a sign on his desk saying "The buck stops here," so people kept coming to him with their problems, like whether to nuke Japan and what to do about Communism, and he hardly had time to catch his breath.

He wrote himself a memo, in case he forgot, saying the White House was a great white jail and "Why in hell does anybody want to be a head of state? Damned if I know." Later on he got used to it, though, and liked it better.

In fact, he got so cocky that in 1947 he built a balcony behind the pillars of the south portico, and you should have heard Washington holler. You'd have thought he'd painted the whole building green. It wasn't the last of their troubles, either, because by fall Harry noticed that his bathtub was getting lower and lower, and then a chandelier in the Blue Room took to shaking during large receptions, and a leg of Margaret's grand piano punched a hole in the dining room ceiling, and the great staircase started to sway, and the whole family prudently moved across the street to Blair House.

---

[4] Later she did take their advice and wrote books instead, and her reviews improved somewhat.

[5] At his first press conference he said, "Boys, if you ever pray, pray for me now."

A committee came to check out the place, and then *they* rushed back outside again. It seemed the footings were only eight feet deep, in squishy clay, and nothing but a natural feeling of respect had kept the building upright ever since we'd stuck on that heavy third floor in 1927. For a while it looked as if the whole pile of rubble ought to be given a gentle push and allowed to fall down, which would have been cheaper in the long run, but sentimentalists prevailed and we propped up the outside walls and built a whole new inside, while the Trumans stayed in Blair House.

By now it was time to decide whether Harry was going to get elected on his own in 1948, or even nominated. Various key Democrats who weren't from Missouri thought he should just resign and go back to Missouri, and the Republicans went around saying "To err is Truman," and thought themselves frightfully funny. The Democrats asked everyone in town if they'd like to run for President instead of Truman, but they all said sorry, they were busy.[6] The Progressives went off and ran Henry Wallace instead, and the Southern Democrats said they were really Dixiecrats and ran Strom Thurmond of South Carolina, who was still grumbling about states' rights and threatening to fire on Fort Sumter. The Republicans got Thomas Dewey again. He was still wearing that ridiculous little black mustache that Alice Roosevelt Longworth said made him look like the bridegroom on a wedding cake, but for some reason everyone thought he'd win anyway, and started calling him "President Dewey." This made them look pretty silly later, though not half as silly as the *Chicago Tribune* running that "Dewey Elected" headline in the early edition. But I'm getting ahead of my story.

---

[6] Both parties wanted General Eisenhower, but he was out on the golf course and couldn't be reached.

Truman was the only person in the whole country who thought he was going to win.[7] He packed up Bess and Margaret and went on a whistle-stop campaign to four hundred towns and cities, and told people there was going to be a Fair Deal, and it wasn't *his* fault the Republican Congress was a bunch of you-know-whats. Folks took to shouting "Give 'em hell, Harry!" so naturally his language got more and more colorful. He could really fry a person's ears off, that Harry.

As you may have already guessed, when he woke up the next morning he was still President and everyone else was embarrassed. Apparently some people had voted for him because he was spunky and just plain folks, while others simply couldn't bring themselves to vote for a man with a ridiculous little black mustache.

Well, now that we didn't have Hitler to worry about, we took to worrying about Communism. Roosevelt had never lost any sleep over it and thought the Russians were okay, but Truman was all for something called "containment." This meant that Communists had to stay bottled up in Russia where they belonged, but we could go anywhere because we were the good guys. We put NATO together to make sure the Communists stayed bottled, and suddenly realized this whole peace business wasn't a good thing after all but a Communist plot to catch us with our guns unloaded.

Then Senator Joseph McCarthy (R., Wisconsin) jumped up and said the Communists weren't staying bottled at all, they were all over *this* country, disguised as people, and he had lists and lists and *lists* of them that he'd show us, only he'd left them in the pocket of his other suit. The House

---

[7] His mother-in-law, a dreadful woman who insisted on living with them and refused to die until 1952, told everyone Dewey was a sure thing.

Un-American Activities Committee said *they* had over a million names, and besides, there were secret messages about peace hidden in movies, history books, plays, folk songs, *Dick Tracy, Prince Valiant,* and the minutes of the Audubon Society meetings.

Everyone had to sign loyalty oaths that they weren't planning to overthrow the government, and if they were, they had to report to their local FBI office and register and get fingerprinted, and the McCarran Act provided for concentration camps to send them to. Nervous types took to jumping out of high windows before explaining themselves to the Committee.

Truman thought it was all poppycock. He called the House Un-American Activities Committee an un-American activity, and said, "All this howl about organizations a fellow belongs to gives me a pain in the neck."[8]

In 1950 there was a local dust-up in Korea. Some say our buddies the South Koreans may have started it, with a little coaching from their American advisors, but the North Koreans were Communists, so we sent General MacArthur over to contain them. Truman said it wasn't a *war,* exactly, just a police action, and not to worry. When we charged clear up to the Chinese border the Chinese, who were also Communists by now, got excited and sent *their* troops in. MacArthur wanted to invade China, which is always a foolish thing to do. Others have tried it in the past. It's too big, and there are too many Chinese. The troops start out all right at the edges, but they take a wrong turn somewhere west of Wuhan and nobody ever sees them again. Their descendants look Chinese.

---

[8] Right away *his* name went on a lot of lists. Nixon said he'd "covered up this Communist conspiracy and attempted to halt its exposure."

Truman sent MacArthur his pink slip and told him to come straight home.[9] This was unpopular, as many believed the sooner we went to war and killed all the Communists everywhere, the better.[10] For starters, we put Julius and Ethel Rosenberg in the electric chair for stealing atomic secrets for the Russians. Scientists found this a terrific giggle because there weren't any atomic secrets and never had been, and any fool with a spoonful of uranium could cook up an atom bomb in his kitchen. After a while a lot of foreign countries started doing just that, with no help at all from the Rosenbergs. Our feelings were hurt. Whose bomb was it, anyway?

I forget how the Korea business ended. Actually, I'm not sure it did end, but after a long time it sort of stopped.

Truman said he'd done his damndest and didn't want to be President any more, which was just as well. The Republicans said he stood for "Korea, Communism, and Corruption," and many Democrats agreed, though some later decided he'd really been better at being President than at selling shirts and ties.

There are historians who think Truman shouldn't have dropped those things on Japan. They say it was childish and irresponsible and Japan was all ready to surrender anyway, and some critics go so far as to call it the most heinous[11] decision ever made by an American President. Truman him-

---

[9] He said he did it because MacArthur was insubordinate, not because he was "a dumb son-of-a-bitch," although he was.

[10] The Russians were feeling the same way about us. Folks took to calling this the Cold War, and printed bumper stickers saying "Better Dead Than Red," and sat around fidgeting and trying to read in stuffy bomb shelters in the backyard waiting for the end of the world.

[11] "Heinous" is a word critics like to use because it sounds so final, especially if you know how to pronounce it. It is usually saved up to use on people like Hitler.

self felt quite cheerful about it.[12] After all, we were fighting a war, and it was a bomb, wasn't it? What were we supposed to *do* with the thing if not drop it—put place mats on it and call it a tea table?

Right or wrong, the bomb didn't go away afterward, and neither did all those Communists. History now came to a stop and the modern world began. No one has quite decided whether this is a good thing or not.

------

[12] When the atomic scientists wrung their hands over it, Harry said, "This kind of sniveling makes me sick."

Dwight David Eisenhower

1953–1961

★

isenhower, or Ike, was President for eight years and nothing happened. This was just fine with most people and it was fine with Ike too. He'd been busy as a beaver with the war and now it was time to take things easy. He was fond of golf and bridge.

Ike didn't look much like a general. He had a round bald head and a cheerful smile and he looked like a happy door-knob.[1] He came from Abilene, Kansas, and graduated from West Point sixty-first in a class of 164, which was better than Grant, anyway. He won the war in Europe while MacArthur was winning the war in the Pacific. His wife's name was Mamie.

Ike was confused but kindly, and he didn't know diddley-do about politics. He'd never been much of a one for voting. He said, "Nothing in the international or domestic situation especially qualifies for the most important office in the world a man whose adult life has been spent in the military forces."[2]

When the Republicans finally got his attention and asked him to run for President anyway, he said he'd only do it if *both* parties wanted him. This is not the way it usually works, so Adlai Stevenson ran against him. Stevenson was governor of Illinois, and an intellectual with a famous hole in the sole of his shoe. He lost badly.[3]

The most exciting thing about the campaign was Nixon. He was going to be Vice-President, and was already famous for exposing disguised Communists, particularly the ones

---

[1] MacArthur, now, *there* was a general who looked like a general. He tried to get nominated in '48 and '52 but nothing came of it. You can look *too* much like a general.

[2] He often got so wound up in his sentences that his aides had to rush over and untangle him before he choked to death. It was kind of cute.

[3] Next time he lost worse.

who were running for office against him. Then some Nosy Parkers wanted to hear what he'd done with a bunch of money people had given him. All sorts of clamor got clamored, and Ike wouldn't say anything one way or the other. He just smiled. So Nixon had to spend seventy-five thousand dollars of the National Committee's money for television time so he could make his Checkers speech. (See Appendix III.) I can't find out who wrote it but it was a corker, and everyone cried and hugged, and Ike and Dick won in a landslide.[4]

The inside of the White House was back in business, and Mamie had a lot of it painted pink. She liked pink carnations too. Pink was her favorite color. In the evenings she and Ike liked to watch television, or have some folks over for bridge. They'd moved thirty times in thirty-six years, and it was nice just to sit around for a change.

John Foster Dulles was Secretary of State, and he tried hard to make things more exciting but Ike wouldn't let him. Dulles wanted to free the Eastern European countries from the Russians. He wanted to "unleash" poor old Chiang Kaishek from where he'd been vegetating and picking at his cuticles on Taiwan, and go free Red China from the Red Chinese and give it back to him. He made up the "domino theory" and explained it to Ike, how if one country went Communist, then all their neighbors and then *their* neighbors would go Communist too. He was interested in the new hydrogen bomb for some industrial-strength Communistcontaining.

Ike just smiled.[5]

---

[4] All right, then, it wasn't *very* exciting, but it seemed exciting at the time. It was a quiet time.

[5] He never felt at home with those newfangled weapons anyway, the ones he called "nucular." He was strictly a guns-and-tanks man himself.

He never worried much. When people handed him worrying papers to read, he just smiled and handed them right back. He didn't even worry about Senator McCarthy. He pretended there wasn't any Senator McCarthy. When people mentioned McCarthy he just blinked and got in his helicopter and went out to Burning Tree to play a few holes before dinner. He figured if he didn't pay any attention to McCarthy then McCarthy would just go away, and presently the Senate got fed up and censured the gentleman from Wisconsin and he did go away, sputtering and fumbling with his lists and still needing a shave, so Ike was right not to worry.

In 1957 the Russians sent up the Sputnik satellite, and in 1959 Castro took over Cuba. When it was too rainy for golf Ike did some oil painting, but he never got very good at it.[6] When the rain stopped he went out and putted a few on his putting green at the edge of the White House lawn. The squirrels gave him a hard time and he tried to have them all trapped and taken somewhere else, but there are always fresh supplies of squirrels. You can't get rid of *all* the squirrels, and it's foolish to even try.

People liked having Ike in the White House because he made them feel safe and warm all over. He would have been a cinch for a third term and maybe a fourth, except that the Republicans had been afraid Roosevelt might not be dead after all and passed the Twenty-second Amendment, which says that twice is enough. Didn't they just kick themselves, too.

---

[6] To be frank, he was even worse than Churchill.

John Fitzgerald Kennedy

1961–1963

★

The Kennedy administration was so short that some historians call it an interlude instead. Fans call it Camelot, after King Arthur's headquarters, also a famous center for knights-errant, highfalutin ideals, parties, and romantic canoodling in the corridors. King Arthur had it easier, though. He may have had Guinevere, but he didn't have Congress.

Jack Kennedy was pushed into politics as a second-string substitute for his brother Joe Jr., the family jewel, who was killed in the war, and don't think Joe Sr. let Jack forget it for a minute. Joe Jr. had always been better and bigger and stronger than Jack.[1] When they were kids he'd pounded Jack to a pulp, and later danced off with his dates whenever he'd a mind to.

Sometimes Jack got to feeling Joe Jr. had come back disguised as Russia. This made him feisty and led to enterprises like the Bay of Pigs and the Cuban Missile Crisis, giving rise to the word "brinkmanship," and competitions like the Space Race. Jack hated coming in second. His father always told him that it wasn't so much how you played the game as whether you won or lost, and if you lost you got sent to bed without supper.[2]

He'd always thought he'd be a writer, and he was, too. His senior thesis at Harvard was published as *Why England Slept* and made the best-seller list. So did *Profiles in Courage,* and it won a Pulitzer too. But nobody said no to Joe Sr. and off Jack went to Congress when he was only twenty-nine and looked about twelve.

It was a cinch. To start with, he was a genuine war hero.

---

[1] Jack was such a sickly child that his family said if a mosquito bit him and got a drop of his blood, then it was curtains for the mosquito.

[2] If you were beating Jack at checkers, he'd tip the board over and pretend it was an accident.

When his PT-109 got rammed and sunk, his back, which had been tricky for years anyway, was seriously smashed, but he hauled out all ten survivors and swam them to an island miles away, all the time towing a wounded man with his teeth sunk into the fellow's life preserver. Top *that*. Besides, both his grandfathers had been Irish Democratic bosses in Boston, and Honey Fitz had been mayor, too.

As soon as Jack was old enough he moved up to the Senate. A highlight of that campaign was the night he and brothers Bobby and Teddy all stood on the table at the G&G Deli and sang "Heart of My Heart." Who could resist?

Came the Democratic convention of 1960. Skeptics said no Catholic could ever get elected,[3] and remember the pasting Al Smith took in '28, and why not have Lyndon Johnson, Senate Majority Leader, instead? But Jack made it on the first ballot, and said Lyndon could be his running mate. In his acceptance speech he told people there were New Frontiers all over—science, space, peace, war, ignorance, poverty, etc., etc.—and we'd all have to pitch in and do something about them. Nobody paid much mind until the debates.

Kennedy and Nixon argued with each other on television programs specially arranged for the purpose, and Nixon fans claim their boy lost the election because of his makeup man. They said with the right makeup man, Nixon could have been *every bit* as sexy as Kennedy. Nixon always needed a shave, out of respect for his fellow Commie-spotter Senator McCarthy, who always needed a shave too. The makeup man tried to cover the stubble with a special heavy-duty face

---

[3] While Jack was President many insisted that he was digging a tunnel from the White House basement straight to the Vatican. This would have been expensive and impractical. Couldn't he just pick up the phone?

powder, but it didn't work.[4] Also the lighting did sinister things to his eye sockets. One historian said, "He looked for all the world like a man with shaving and perspiration problems, glumly waiting for the commercial to tell him how not to offend."

The debates were mostly over what to do about a couple of islands off the coast of Taiwan.[5] This may have seemed more urgent at the time than it does now. In any case Kennedy won the debates and the election, but it was such a close squeak that it didn't give him much clout with Congress.

Robert Frost wrote a special poem for the inauguration, but the sunlight was so bright and squinty he couldn't read it. This was just as well. It was dreadful slop. Kennedy's speech was a rouser, though, and the recording later sold millions as a 45 single. He said, "Ask not what your country can do for you; ask what you can do for your country."

Countless Americans had slipped away from their offices and repaired to the nearest pub to watch television, and when they heard this they rushed out onto the sidewalk with their beer mugs sloshing over their knuckles and peered up and down the street looking for something to do for their country. There wasn't anything in sight, so they went back to their offices.[6]

Ernest Hemingway said, "It is a good thing to have a brave man as our President in times as tough as these are."

A senator said, "He seems to combine the best qualities of Elvis Presley and Franklin D. Roosevelt."

John Steinbeck said, "What a joy that literacy is no longer prima-facie evidence of treason."

A top aide said, "This administration is going to do for sex what the last one did for golf."

---

[4] As of this writing, there is still no real substitute for a shave.
[5] I'd tell you their names, but you'd only forget.
[6] By and by it turned out they could go fight in Vietnam.

Kennedy had a photogenic wife named Jackie who spoke French and rode horses[7] and two photogenic children named Caroline and John-John, and he didn't break any lenses himself, even in bathing trunks. In nice weather they all joined hundreds of other tanned and fit Kennedys at the family compound in Hyannisport and made the guests play touch football. The Kennedys played a hard-nosed game.[8] Important guests staggered home exhausted and frightened, saying to watch out for the women because even eight months pregnant they're faster than you are. It was kind of like TR chasing the ambassadors through Rock Creek Park, only there were so many more Kennedys. They were everywhere, even in the Cabinet, and non-Kennedys began to feel paranoid and outnumbered.

In the White House Jackie found things had gotten terribly unsophisticated under the Trumans and Eisenhowers, so she hired a French chef, and dusted off the punch bowls of state, and had music and dancing in the East Room, and Nobel prize-winners, and performances of Shakespeare. She called in a Fine Arts Committee and fixed the place up with antiques and some better-looking pictures. She rummaged around and found a sofa of Dolley Madison's and that carved oak desk Queen Victoria sent to Rutherford B. Hayes, and kept pushing the stuff around until she got it just right. Then she went on television and showed all of us. It looked fine.

The Kennedys had a Welsh terrier named Charlie, and Caroline had a pony named Macaroni, who followed visitors around the lawn, and two hamsters named Bluebell and Marybelle. Nikita Khrushchev gave them a dog named Pu-

---

[7] American men often said they could identify with Kennedy better than with the previous administration, because who wanted to go to bed with Mamie? This was very rude of them and quite uncalled-for.

[8] Jack was serious about fitness and told everyone on his staff to lose five pounds or leave.

shinka, offspring of Strelka, the first dog in orbit. It had to have its ears probed for electronic bugs. Joe Sr. gave them a German shepherd named Clipper. Reporters asked Jackie what she was going to feed it and Jackie said, "Reporters."

Intellectuals thought it was exciting that we were finally getting some intellectuals around here. Jack hired a performing troupe of Rhodes scholars and Phi Beta Kappas to help run things. He read newspapers to find out what was happening. He could read two thousand words a minute, giving him the jump on most Presidents, and tore through four morning papers in fifteen minutes flat, even with the children racing around underfoot.

He and some other Kennedys thought up the Peace Corps, under which earnest Americans went off to the Third World to teach it useful skills like English and digging latrines.[9] He tried to do all sorts of New Frontier things, like Medicare, and aid to education, and a civil rights bill, but somehow nothing much happened except that he single-handedly destroyed the men's hat industry by refusing to wear a hat. Congress just shrugged and ignored him.

He had better luck in other countries, where people found him and Jackie far more dashing than previous samples of American leadership, even if he did do some scatty things in Cuba. In France he introduced himself as "the man who accompanied Jackie Kennedy to Paris." In West Berlin he said he was a Berliner too, only he said it in German. The crowds just ate it up.

His daughter Caroline called him Silly Daddy. His son John-John called him Foo-Foo Head. Jackie called him Bunny. Some of his friends called him Jack the Zipper—they didn't explain why.

In Dallas, on November 22, 1963, three hours before he

---

[9] Many of them wound up marrying each other, and were twice as earnest afterward.

was shot, he said, "If anybody really wanted to shoot the President . . . it is not a very difficult job. . . . Get on a high building some day with a telescopic rifle and there is nothing anyone can do to defend against such an attempt."[10]

Afterward the Warren Commission went back and forth over the whole thing, with the aid of some home movies taken by a helpful fellow named Abraham Zapruder, who'd remembered to bring his camera, and decided Lee Harvey Oswald shot him from the Texas School Book Depository. Others disagreed and dragged up complicated questions about the number of bullets and which directions they were traveling through Kennedy and Governor Connally, who was sitting next to him, and in a twinkling who-shot-Kennedy became a leading industry accounting for a significant percentage of the GNP. Suspects included, but were not limited to, Oswald, who got shot by Jack Ruby before he could say anything, the FBI, the CIA, the Mafia, the Fair Play for Cuba Committee, Jack Ruby, who shot Oswald before he could say anything, a Mr. Clay Shaw, Vice-President Johnson, and an unidentified man in a sort of police uniform who was walking across the grassy knoll.[11]

Funnily enough, three years later, eighteen of the key witnesses were dead, including two suicides. Somebody with nothing better to do figured out that the odds against this mortality rate were one hundred thousand trillion to one, give or take a couple.

Jackie stayed up all night and made the funeral arrangements and refused to change her clothes. She was wearing

---

[10] This is the kind of thing collectors of the strange and marvelous are just potty about and keep repeating to each other. I don't see what's so special about it myself. He may have said it every time he went outdoors. Who wouldn't?

[11] The grassy knoll grew so famous some folks got confused and thought it was a suspect too.

a pink suit that was all spattered with blood but she wouldn't take it off, and for three days she was our first national heroine since Betsy Ross.[12]

At the funeral drums were drummed all day, and little John-John saluted the casket, and everyone cried, even foreigners. Even anchormen.

For a few minutes there, Kennedy had led us to believe we were all of us stylish and witty, merry in heart and terrific in bed, and really *good* people besides. Special people. After he was killed we realized we were just the same old ordinary money-grubbing us we'd always been, and we were a terrible disappointment to ourselves for a while.

Of course, if he hadn't been killed, we'd have realized it sooner or later anyway. These things never last.

---

[12] Later people were hurt and angry that she didn't go on forever being our national heroine, but she felt three days had been plenty. It's hard work.

Lyndon Baines Johnson

1963–1969

★

When the shots rang out in Dallas, which is the proper way to describe the occasion, a Secret Service agent knocked Johnson down to the floor of the car and lay on top of him as a shield—an awkward maneuver since Johnson was six foot three and had to be folded up and *stuffed* onto the floor—and when they untangled their arms and legs and sat up again Johnson was President.

He was the only President ever sworn in on an airplane in Texas, and his first words in office were "Now, let's get airborne." After he got back to Washington, Congress felt so guilty about Kennedy that it passed all those bills he'd set his heart on, about Medicare and education and letting black people eat in restaurants and have jobs.

Johnson started up the Department of Transportation, something the Founding Fathers had overlooked because of not having any. He added Housing and Urban Development, and gave it to Robert Weaver as the first black in the Cabinet. He put Thurgood Marshall on the Supreme Court, too. Ralph Ellison said, "Perhaps President Johnson will have to settle for being recognized as the greatest American President for the poor and for Negroes."[1]

What Johnson really wanted was to be king of something he called The Great Society, where nobody would be hungry or angry or ignorant, and people would like each other and sing happy songs all day. He had big plans for it, only he had trouble getting this Vietnam business out of his hair.

He said, "Just like the Alamo, somebody damned well needed to go to their aid. Well, by God, I'm going to Vietnam's aid."

It wasn't very *much* like the Alamo. Hardly at all, really. It was bigger, for one thing, and full of North and South

---

[1] He's also recognized as having the largest ears of any American President. They looked like the giant tree-fungi from hell, and made the political cartoonists very, very happy.

Vietnamese, Ho Chi Minh, and places with funny names like Num Dong. Besides, the Alamo was over in ten days, and the war in Vietnam had already been going on for ten years and showed no signs of fatigue.

So every time he tried to think about his Great Society, there was Vietnam whining around his ears like a mosquito in the bedroom. It was a great nuisance, and it got worse, too.

When Johnson was born in Stonewall, Texas, his grand-daddy said, "He'll be a United States senator some day." This responsibility so weighed on his parents that it took them three months to think of a name for him, and then the best they could come up with was "Lyndon." He was often called LBJ, after his ranch in the Texas Pedernales.[2] He had his wife and daughters answer to Lady Bird, Lynda Bird, and Luci Baines, so they could all have the same initials as the ranch.[3]

Lyndon knew the alphabet by the time he was two and was reading up a storm at four. He graduated from high school at fifteen as president of his class, because the other six kids didn't want to be president and he did. (He always did.) After Southwest Texas State College he taught public speaking for a while and then went to Washington as secretary to Congressman Kleberg. Roosevelt took a shine to him and made him the Texas straw boss of the National Youth Administration, administrating youths, and pretty soon he turned up in Congress. In '41 he was the first congressman to enlist, and just had time to grab a Silver Star before Roosevelt told all the congressmen in uniform to quit playing soldier and come home and get back to work. In '49 he

_____

[2] He was also called "King Lyndon" and "Uncle Cornpone." Kennedy aides called him "The Great Guided Missile." (He called *them* "The Georgetown Jellybeans.")

[3] Presently the girls got married and spoiled everything.

went to the Senate, just like his granddaddy said, and he was Majority Leader when Kennedy whistled for him.

In the beginning he had a great time being President and handed out ten-gallon hats to visitors. In 1964 he walked into the Democratic Convention and everybody there stood up and burst into "Hello, Lyndon" to something like the tune of "Hello, Dolly." It was the most dismal racket you ever heard but it showed they liked him. He and Hubert Humphrey ran against Barry Goldwater and carried forty-four states, with a walloping 61 percent of the popular vote.[4]

To start with he had a Democratic Congress, and when he told them to haul off and pass a law, they said "Yessir," which was what he liked to hear. Lady Bird said she'd married him because "sometimes Lyndon simply takes your breath away." Others complained about this too. He had a lot of energy.

People went around telling each other Johnson stories. It didn't seem to matter whether they were true or not because they were all pretty much the same story.

Sample #1: At the airport an army sergeant sees Johnson heading for the wrong helicopter, and he goes up to him and says, "Excuse me, Mr. President, but that's your helicopter over there." Johnson beams and throws an arm over the sergeant's shoulders and says, "Son, they're *all* my helicopters."

Sample #2: A Texas state trooper chases a car doing around a hundred and ten. When it finally pulls over, the trooper strides up to it and looks in the driver's window and recognizes his victim. "Oh, my God," he says. Johnson says, "That's right, sonny, and don't you forget it."

If you want any more you can make up your own.

People would have gone right on liking him because he

---

[4] I suppose this might say something about Barry Goldwater, too.

was kind of like Andy Jackson, noisy and bossy but real down-home, and we don't mind people thinking they're king as long as they don't put on airs. Johnson wouldn't have known airs if they'd blown his hat off, and he invited folks over to the ranch and served a chili that made your shoes smoke.[5] Sensitive people said he shouldn't pick up his beagles, Him and Her, by their ears, but he said they liked it. Prudes said he shouldn't pull up his shirt and show off the scars on his tummy for the press, but the press said they liked it. He was fun to read about and this is always the main thing.

There was this war, though. It wasn't at all like World War II, because it didn't have Hitler, and besides, most people knew where Europe was and nobody knew where Vietnam was, even after they'd been there for years. They started to resent having to go die in a country they couldn't find on the map.[6]

Suddenly students on both coasts took to letting their hair grow clear down their backs, abusing substances, writing significant folk songs about peace, and burning their draft cards if they were boys and their bras if they were girls until the air was quite blue with smoke. In the Seventies, this was known as The Sixties. It wasn't a bit what Johnson meant by The Great Society and he was pretty miffed.

He lost Congress, too. It filled up with Republicans, and they got busy and took his Great Society money away from the social programs and sent it off to the war. From time to time there were riots. The whole country divided up into

---

[5] Lady Bird had a terrific recipe for spoonbread, too. You should try it.

[6] Some thought it was really Korea, because of having places with funny names and good guys in the south and bad guys in the north, but it wasn't. It was south of Korea. For all I know, it still is.

two teams, the Hawks, who thought we should keep fighting till the last Commie bit the dust, and the Doves, who floated around with irritating smiles and poked daisies into the business ends of rifles. The only thing they agreed on was that they didn't like Johnson anymore. The Hawks thought a half million troops in Vietnam wasn't half enough and the Doves thought it was a half million too many.[7]

Johnson got so irritable there was no living with him. In his dreams he thought even his best friends were out to get him. Then he started thinking they were out to get him when he was awake, too. He kept saying he couldn't trust anyone. Sometimes he heard planes coming in to land at National and thought they were coming to drop bombs on him.

In March of '68 he said all right, if that's the way we felt about it, then he wouldn't run for reelection, so there. He said maybe if he just went away we'd all stop quarreling and be friends again. In November he stopped the bombing in Vietnam, and peace talks started.[8]

In January he gave Nixon the door key and went home.[9]

Nothing ever did come of the Great Society, but Lady Bird had planted daffodils all along Rock Creek Parkway, and they're still there, and in the spring they look very nice indeed. They seem kind of *cozier* than the cherry blossoms, if you know what I mean.

---

[7] This would have led to arguments at dinner parties, only Hawks and Doves never got invited to the same parties.

[8] False alarm. Sorry.

[9] Halfway through FDR, new Presidents had taken to starting work in January instead of March, so the weather for the parade was even worse, if possible.

Richard Milhous Nixon

1969–1974

★

There's a lot to be said about Nixon. Nixon himself said a lot about Nixon, since whenever he didn't have time to write books and memos and speeches about himself, he was recording every word he uttered on tape, for posterity, a practice he had second thoughts about later. He was his own favorite subject, and if you want to know a whole lot more about him than you already know, well then, there's a whole lot more out there waiting for you. If you laid it all end to end, you'd be surprised.

Some people liked Nixon and some people didn't, but say what you will, he was definitely our manliest President. You could see it in the navy-blue jowls. His language was so manly it was around 40 percent unprintable and made Truman sound like a nun, and all his acquaintances were manly too. Even his worst enemies could never prove that, aside from siring two children, he ever had anything at all to do with women. The closest thing to a sex scandal in his administration was when he and a couple of buddies were out on the yacht, and they'd brought along a life-sized, female-shaped inflatable doll. They kept hiding this doll in each other's beds, frightening each other out of their wits and laughing themselves sick.[1] You have to admit it was pretty funny.

He did have a wife called Pat,[2] and sometimes he remembered this and sometimes he didn't. Sometimes he forgot to introduce her to people even when she was standing right there with her hand stuck out, or absentmindedly went home from the party alone and left her behind looking foolish. When he thought she should know about something, he

---

[1] The Kennedys, who were always hanging around with a bunch of women, put real girls in their beds, and let them get lipstick on their shirt collars and hang stockings over the shower-curtain rod. You're either manly or you're just not.
[2] Her real name was Thelma Catherine, if you must know.

sent a memo to one of his aides to go tell her. In emergencies he'd even send her a memo directly, like about the end table by the bed, and how it had to be bigger because "RN has to use one dictaphone for current matters and another for memoranda," and besides, the bedroom worktable "does not allow enough room for him to get his knees under it." She was used to this and knew right away who RN was without even stopping to wonder. Sometimes, in the White House, they'd have dinner together, if he remembered and wasn't busy or off in the Bahamas or Camp David with his buddies, or if photographers were coming. I have no idea what they talked about.

Pat seemed like a nice woman with a slightly stunned expression, and avoided interviews. She'd had a tough life earlier but never quite like this.

Nixon had been manly since earliest childhood.[3] A schoolmate remembered, "Oh, he used to dislike us girls so! ... As a debater, his main theme in grammar school and the first years of high school was why he hated girls." Nothing in later life altered his opinion. He preferred playing poker and talking about football and running for office, especially against effeminate pinkos like Helen Gahagan Douglas.[4] Whenever he thought about pinkos and perverts his testosterone shot right off the charts and his beard grew half an inch.[5]

Nixon was born in a lemon grove and grew up in southern California, but if you're trying to imagine him sprinting

---

[3] His mother named him after Richard the Lion-Hearted, who was famous for his battles with his father, his brothers, the Saracens, and anyone else he could poke a sword into. He wasn't home much either.

[4] All he had to do was call her "The Pink Lady." It worked like a charm.

[5] Later on, reporters had the same effect on him.

across the beach with a surfboard on his head, pursued by shrieking blondes in bikinis, I don't recommend it. Not without some preliminary warm-up exercise, like imagining Woodrow Wilson in a gorilla suit.

He went to Whittier College and then to Duke University Law School. Everyone called him "Gloomy Gus." This was a joke, probably. He didn't have much luck as a young lawyer, so he tried to sell frozen orange juice in little plastic bags, but who wants to drink orange juice out of a bag? He joined the navy. When he came home he was manlier than ever and trounced the congressional incumbent by calling him a "lip-service American . . . fronting for un-American elements." He was the first to point out to voters that secret pinkos are wily, and naturally the wily thing to do is to sound and vote like conservative anti-Communists, which is how you can tell they're secret pinkos. This revolutionized American politics for years to come.

He settled right down in Congress to become the shining light of the House Un-American Activities Committee, where he was the only person who believed Whittaker Chambers when he said Alger Hiss was a secret pinko.[6] Hiss went to jail, and Nixon moved up to the Senate and on to be Ike's Vice-President.

Ike often sent Nixon off traveling around the world, and then went out to play golf.[7] Nixon would come home from these goodwill tours with spit and vegetables all over his suit, and Ike would let him wash up and then send him off somewhere else. In 1956 Ike suggested that he look around for another job, but Nixon wasn't listening and went right

---

[6] He figured pretty much everyone else was, so why not Hiss?
[7] He thought Nixon was a giant pain. He wouldn't show him where the Oval Office was and avoided him as much as possible, which was pretty much. That may have been what he was doing out on the golf course.

on being Vice-President and going places. He went clear to Russia to give Khrushchev a piece of his mind and tell him how much manlier we were than the Russians. Khrushchev said Nixon didn't "know anything about Communism—except fear," which was ridiculous as Nixon was our national authority on Communism, and when he came home he was a national hero too.

Ike couldn't be President again, so Nixon ran instead. You remember the debates with Kennedy? You remember he lost? Well, he always hated losing, so he went back to California and ran for governor, and lost *again.* He could hardly believe it. He was *furious.* He charged up to the reporters all rumpled and sputtering, and said, "You won't have Nixon to kick around any more because, gentlemen, this is my last press conference!" Bystanders thought he was having a nervous breakdown, but he said no, he was perfectly cool inside, he was *always perfectly cool.*

A television network ran a special called "The Political Obituary of Richard Nixon." People teased them about it for years.

In 1968 he made a surprise comeback and beat Johnson's Vice-President, Hubert Horatio Humphrey, who hadn't even bothered to change his name. His first official act in the White House was to throw away everything Johnson had ever touched, even the rugs and the telephones, and scrape the paint off the office walls because Johnson had been sitting inside them.

Nixon was not a cuddly President. He liked to go for long manly walks on the beach all by himself, wearing black business shoes and black socks pulled clear up to his knees. He never, ever unbuttoned his suit jacket, so that when he threw his arms up in his favorite public greeting, it climbed up his neck and swallowed his head, and his tailor buried his face in his hands and moaned. Right from the start he referred to himself as "The President," because he thought it had more of a ring to it than "Nixon" or "me," which it does. When an old friend called him "Dick," he said, "I am the President of the United States! When you speak to me you call me 'Mr. President.' " In fact, he didn't much like people speaking to him at all. Sometimes when he was off relaxing with his buddies, none of them spoke for days.

You mustn't think he didn't have his sentimental side, though. He was just crazy about a nice fire in the fireplace, for instance, and sometimes he built up such a cozy blaze that alarms went off and firemen rushed in. In July and August he turned the air-conditioning down to super-freeze, and *then* he built a nice fire in the fireplace.

Vietnam was still going on and on. Sometimes The President said he had a secret plan for stopping it, and sometimes he said peace was at hand, and sometimes he just bombed it a lot harder. Nothing seemed to work. Students let their hair grow even longer and camped out on the Mall muttering discontentedly.

To take our minds off it we went to the moon. This was in July of '69, and Neil Armstrong and "Buzz" Aldrin got out of the spaceship and walked around on the actual moon, making footprints. The President rang them up on a special telephone and said, "Because of what you have done the heavens have become part of man's world."

Well, they hadn't, really, but it was fun at the time. It really was. We'd been feeling kind of closed in down here, now that we'd found out what was in places like central Africa and Marie Byrd Land, and here was a whole new place to go, and we were all excited. Then it turned out that it was specialized work, going to the moon, and nobody was going to send *us* up there to jump around in the funny gravity making footprints and peer down at the world and try to find our houses, and if we were going anywhere it would probably be the same old hotel in Ocean City with the same old sand in the beds. By and by we all stopped thinking about it and went back to feeling closed in.

In '72 The President and his peculiar Vice-President, Spiro Agnew, beat George McGovern.[8] This was called "Four More Years," because at the time people still thought Watergate was just an apartment building.

Early in '73 Henry Kissinger, The President's international branch office, managed to stop us from fighting in Vietnam. Then we took to bombing Cambodia instead, because we still had bombs left over and who could tell the Cambodians from the Vietnamese anyway?

Finally it was time for Watergate. It seems that during the previous election The President's people had been so staunch and loyal and fond of The President that they'd done some things a person could misinterpret, like burgling the Democratic headquarters in Watergate, and some nosy reporters had to go and make a big deal out of it. The President said *he* didn't have anything to do with it, because he was too busy thinking about affairs of state to think about getting reelected, let alone burgling, and besides, he was somewhere else at the time, and no, nobody could go poking through his memos and tape recordings for evidence because he was The President. He said he'd *tell* the Senate and the special prosecutor what was on the tapes, if they really wanted to know, but the whole thing was simply ridiculous. As an afterthought he fired the special prosecutor, but wouldn't you know another special prosecutor popped up?

As if The President didn't have enough on his mind, it turned out that Spiro Agnew, the peculiar Vice-President, had been sticking to some little envelopes all full of money he was hard-pressed to explain and had to quit quite suddenly, leaving his desk a mess. The President had to knock off work early and go over to the Hill and pick out a new Vice-President. It's always something.

The House Judiciary Committee had no sense of humor

---

[8] Some people can never remember which was McGovern and which was Mondale. It doesn't matter.

and was making a federal case out of the Watergate caper.[9] In July of '74 they recommended impeaching The President three times, once for trying to stop us from finding out about Watergate, once for doing things Presidents shouldn't, and once for not answering the door when people came pounding on it with subpoenas. The President said all right, all right, we could *have* the f——g tapes, or some of them, or parts of some of them, if that's the way we felt. Well, it turned out that recording your every word isn't always the bright idea it seems like, even if you're The President and every word's important. Many people were more upset by The President's vocabulary than they were by Watergate, and various key Republicans suggested he start packing because things could get a whole lot worse.

He announced his departure on August 8, the 162nd anniversary of Napoleon getting punted off to languish on St. Helena. The Dow-Jones went up twenty-seven points. Historian Henry Steele Commager said, "Other things being equal, we haven't had a *bad* President before now. Mr. Nixon is the first dangerous and wicked President."

As soon as it wasn't on television any more we all stopped wallowing in Watergate and began to forget all about it, and in a few years Nixon started turning into an elder statesman. He wrote manly books about himself and foreign policy, himself and Southeast Asia, and himself and world peace. Serious people clustered around him and asked him deep questions, like what he thought about China, because he'd

---

[9] The President called this "wallowing in Watergate," and urged us all to cut it out before he put us on the Enemies List and sent us tax auditors and parking tickets and dead mice in the mailbox. We went right on wallowing. We couldn't help it. It was on radio and television every day, and it was even more fun than the moon landing and lasted even longer than "Upstairs, Downstairs."

spent a week there in '72 and this is more than most of us have spent. They all agreed that Watergate had been a splendid chance for the children to learn about the Constitution, and besides, Nixon had made it okay to be a right-wing Republican again for the first time since Hoover, and if it hadn't been for Nixon we might not have had any Ronald Reagan, and how would you like *that*?

Gerald Rudolph Ford, Jr.

1974–1977

★

On the very first morning that Ford was President, he came to his front door in his blue-and-white striped pajamas and reached out to pick up his morning paper and looked around, and bless us, the yard was full of reporters and cameramen and he was all embarrassed.

When the American public heard this they were overcome by a great wash of relief. In the typical subject this sensation began somewhere at the back of the neck and spread slowly in a warm tide down to the soles of the feet: *Here was a President we didn't have to think about.* We were *tired* of thinking about the President. We'd been thinking about Richard Nixon, man and boy, for twenty-six years, since HUAC days, and day and night for over two years, and now we wanted to think about ourselves for a change, and when Gerry Ford came to the door in his pajamas many broke down and wept for joy.[1]

Gerry seemed to be something of a dingbat, and this was a relief too. It was suggested that more than his nose had been damaged on the football field. Lyndon Johnson said he'd played too often without a helmet and called him "the only man I ever knew who can't fart and chew gum at the same time,"[2] but we didn't care. We all told each other Gerry jokes, because nobody had been able to think of any Nixon jokes.

Then Gerry pardoned Nixon. He said he didn't know what Nixon had done, exactly, that was against the presidential rules, but whatever it was, it was okay and he couldn't ever be punished for it or even asked about it anymore.

Well, naturally the usual cynics thought there'd been hanky-panky. Here Nixon had gone over to the Hill, after

---

[1] Nobody could imagine Nixon coming to the door in his pajamas, or even going to bed in them. It was taken for granted he slept in his suit. Maybe his shoes too.

[2] This statement was altered slightly for publication.

that little problem with Agnew, and picked out what folks called a "spectacularly average congressman" to be Vice-President. Ten months later here's the man President and pardoning Nixon, and the question was, why did he pick Ford? Hinters hinted that he'd lined up rows and rows of Republican congressmen and said, okay, which of you b——ds would pardon The President if the s——t hit the fan? and Ford jumped up, waving his arm and knocking over his chair, and said "Me, sir!" and got the job.[3]

Hey, maybe Nixon just picked Ford because he *looked* like an easy guy with a pardon.[4] Anyway, at the time Nixon wasn't an elder statesman yet, and a few hotheads thought he should go to trial, just to tell us what really happened at Watergate. Others said it wouldn't look right if push came to shove and there was The ex-President of the United States in the pokey getting his breakfast slipped in through a slot, because things like that give the place a bad name. Anyhow, Nixon was pardoned and he stayed pardoned.

Aside from the pardoning, the main controversy of the Ford Regency was just how dumb Gerry really was. Some supporters claimed he was only pretending to be dumb, because *nobody* could be *that* dumb. Journalist Larry L. King said, "He is so average one almost suspects it to be deliberate."[5] An old friend said that instead of trying to outsmart his opponents, he outdumbed them, and this worked just fine, though it's hard to see how, exactly. Some asked how come the loyal voters of Grand Rapids, Michigan, sent him

---

[3] Gerry *liked* Nixon. He said Nixon reminded him a whole lot of Lincoln, and he always ate Nixon's favorite lunch, cottage cheese with plenty of catsup, whenever it was on the menu.

[4] Sometimes, for photographers, Gerry set his jaw and tried to look manly, mostly managing to look like a little boy pretending to be an alligator.

[5] As a child he had a dog named Spot. Honest.

to Congress thirteen times in a row if he was so dumb? (They never got a satisfactory answer.) His wife Betty said, "I think a President has to be able to think like the people think."

It may be that Gerry was just permanently confused. When he was born, his mother named him Leslie Lynch King, Jr., after his father, and then several years later thought it over, divorced King, married Gerald Rudolph Ford, and renamed the kid after *him*. It was a mercy she decided to stay with Ford, but even so this kind of thing can rattle a child. It can make him trip over the furniture in later life, and bean old ladies with golf balls, and turn up for his wedding in one black shoe and one brown one.

The major problem of the Ford Regency was inflation. We were having one of those times when supermarkets hire fleet-footed extra help to run up and down the aisles all day raising prices, and housewives race to stay ahead of them and snatch the cans of soup before they go up another fifty cents. Ford tackled the situation head-on. He had millions and millions of big round buttons printed up that said "W.I.N.," which stood for "Whip Inflation Now," and he promised that if we wore them every time we went out in public, pretty soon prices would stop going up and then slowly but surely start going down. Unfortunately not enough people remembered to wear them—you know how it is when you're dressing in a hurry in the morning—so it didn't work, but it might have.

Now it turned out that over the Vietnam years quite a number of young men of draft age had unaccountably disappeared into foreign countries and stayed there, leaving gaps in the population. The public began to notice, and ask each other, "Where's Eddie? I haven't seen Eddie since '71." So Ford said they could all come home and be pardoned, like Nixon, and not go to jail as draft dodgers if they'd apologize by doing community service. Community service consists of jobs that nobody in his right mind would dream of doing except to stay out of jail, and most of the missing young men told Ford to stick it in his ear and stayed where they were. In April of '75 the war finally stopped,[6] but they still wouldn't come home. By this time they were used to being somewhere else.

The *Mayagüez* was the most exciting thing that happened, and even that didn't last long. It was a U.S. merchant ship that had gotten itself captured at sea by some Cambodians, who were still pretty ticked about being bombed, and Gerry made his alligator face and sent for it back. In the scuffle ninety-one Americans got killed or wounded, but the thirty-nine on the *Mayagüez* were rescued, and we'd definitely showed the Cambodians what was what. It was Gerry's manliest act, but by the following Tuesday everyone had forgotten all about it and gone back to telling Gerry jokes.

Squeaky Fromme and Sara Jane Moore both tried to shoot him and failed completely. They didn't even wing him. They were hysterical types and not from your better class of assassin, but no really reputable assassin could be bothered.

The W.I.N. buttons still hadn't worked and the price of canned soup was still going up, so we didn't elect Gerry for a term as a real President. However, his fans did get together and set up the Gerald R. Ford Museum, which is a treasure trove of memorabilia and well worth the trip to Grand Rapids.[7] I recommend the golf balls, which are autographed by Gerry himself. The last I heard, a package of three sells for $12.95, but they may have gone up.

---

[6] Never mind how. We'll go into that later, maybe.

[7] It's in Michigan; you can't miss it.

Jimmy Carter

1977–1981

★

t's hard to explain to foreigners and small children just why Jimmy Carter was such a joke. You had to be there.

Carter wasn't funny the way Gerry Ford was funny. We *liked* Gerry being funny, because we'd never expected to take him seriously, and besides, he wasn't a real President. We didn't vote for him, he just happened. Carter being funny made us feel cheated.

A quick survey among friends and neighborhood bartenders uncovers a broad spectrum of reasons for Carter's funniness.

1. Peanut farming. This is not a manly occupation, not even if you started out graduating with distinction from the Naval Academy. When your father dies and leaves a peanut farm for you to manage, you should just say no. Raising peanuts is not like raising wheat or cattle. Peanuts are funny.

2. His family. His brother Billy sat around whittlin' and spittin' and manufacturin' Billy Beer, which was such an instant failure that the remaining cans sell to collectors for incredible sums; currently, twelve hundred bucks will get you a six-pack. His sister was religious or psychic or something, and his mother—his *mother*—joined the Peace Corps when she was about a million years old and went to someplace flaky like Africa. His daughter Amy had a Siamese cat instead of a dog. His wife Rosalynn had opinions.

3. Being governor of Georgia. Georgia is not a real place, like Massachusetts or Illinois. Georgia is funny, except for downtown Atlanta, and gives you an accent.

4. He talked funny. (See #3 above.)[1]

5. He liked nature, and the environment, and all those things out there on the wrong side of the windows. He wasn't even manly about it, like Teddy Roosevelt. He

---

[1] A scholarly acquaintance of mine was also offended by the way his lips fit over his teeth.

wanted it left alone. Teddy would have found him awfully soppy.

6. The rabbit. Even *he* thought the rabbit was funny, and actually went around *telling* people how his rowboat had been pursued by a vicious seagoing rabbit, when any sensible pol would have murdered the witnesses and sunk them in the river. Many voters found the rabbit an even worse joke than peanuts. Go out and vote, and what do you get? A President who gets publicly pushed around by rabbits.

7. His sweater. It was a dismal baggy old cardigan, and you know perfectly well he must have had better stuff in his closet. The public has a right to expect a President in civilized clothes. Not Matty Van Buren and the orange necktie, necessarily, but *not that cardigan.*

8. His earnestness. All politicians from sheriff to President are expected to care deeply about a few items, called "issues," chosen for them by the prospective voters; i.e., if the voters care about crime, or car insurance, then the pol cares about crime or car insurance, right through the week after the election. Nobody wants or expects a pol who *really* cares. It's embarrassing and unbusinesslike. Apparently Carter really cared, and about things like pollution, housing for the poor, and peace in the Middle East, wherever that is.[2]

9. His name. Nobody ever thought of him as James, which is a dignified presidential handle. He let us think of him as Jimmy. He *encouraged* us to think of him as Jimmy. Adults named Jimmy are funny.

10. His honesty. Maybe people like to call Lincoln "Honest Abe," but you never caught Lincoln saying the wrong thing just because it was true. Honesty in politicians is a sign of mental deficiency, as in telling an interviewer from *Playboy* that you've lusted in your heart after women you aren't

---

[2] Car insurance has gotten just *appalling,* but did Carter care?

married to.[3] American Presidents are all supposed to be simple, straightforward, hometown folks, but a President who really *is* simple, straightforward, hometown folks is worse than a joke, he's a national humiliation and a dork.

And, of course, funniest of all, the hostages.

For a variety of reasons too Middle Eastern to go into, a bunch of Iranian students cut class and barged into our embassy in Teheran and took fifty-two Americans hostage, and Carter *let* them. Oh, it wasn't that he didn't try to get them back—he kept fiddling around working on this deal and that deal, but he was mostly dealing with the wrong people.[4] All the deals fell through, so he decided we should just go crashing in there and rescue them.

Well, *that* was a joke and a half. There were helicopters that wouldn't even *start,* for heaven's sake, but did Carter get out there with a can of grease and a Phillips screwdriver and start them? No. There was one that did start, and what happened? It bumped into a transport plane and eight of our boys got killed. People spoke wistfully about Nixon, and how *Nixon* would have made those helicopters straighten up and fly right, and how Carter couldn't even get them off the *ground.*

Not only were the hostages still hostages, but now the whole *world* was laughing.

The hostages stayed on and on, playing pinochle and getting bored and depressed. We all sent them Christmas cards, but even that didn't cheer them up. They stayed there for 444 days and didn't get home till the very last day of Carter's presidency.

---

[3] A President should either not lust, like Nixon, or do something about it, like Kennedy. Lusting in your heart annoys all of the voters all of the time.

[4] Iran is like that. It's hard to tell the right people from the wrong people. They all look like Iranians.

It was too late. The election was over.

Foreigners and small children, who never understand jokes, may think Jimmy Carter looked like a thoughtful, decent sort of President who cared about poor people and the outdoors, and lost thirty pounds in the White House from worrying and working late. All I can say to them is, you had to be there. It was a scream. Ask anyone.

Ronald Reagan

1981–1989

★

The question I am most often asked by the inquiring scholars and concerned citizens who cluster on my doorstep daily is, "What actually *did* happen in *Bedtime for Bonzo*?"

Arguably President Reagan's most famous film, *Bedtime for Bonzo* was released in 1951, and addresses the question of environment versus heredity, or whether criminal tendencies are familial in chimpanzees.

President Reagan costars as a brilliant young psychology professor who looks *exactly* the same as he looked in the White House. Oh, maybe his neck wasn't as crisp thirty-five years later, and his sideburns grew maybe half an inch, but otherwise he didn't age a minute. It's uncanny.

As *Bonzo* opens, the university's chimpanzee (Bonzo) is out on a ledge looking suicidal, and his lab professor, Hans, is having a Teutonic fit. Hans has a mustache and a funny accent, and like all Germans he cries "Nein!" a lot in times of stress.

Reagan shows up and undertakes to rescue Bonzo by using psychology on him. Either he or somebody dressed like him balances out on the ledge and then, in closer shots, tries out an assortment of theories. He tries "reverse psychology" by urging the chimp to go ahead and jump, which the chimp promptly does, and ends up dangling by his hands. Then he tries "Gestalt theory," or grabbing Bonzo by the paw, and finally wrestles him in through the window of the lab.

Switch to the dean's office, where Dean Breckinridge has just learned that Reagan's father was a con man known as "Silky Boyd." Silky's ex-cellmate has brought a snapshot of Reagan's mother, though I'm not clear why he took it to the dean.[1] The problem here is that Reagan is engaged to the

---

[1] I'm not even sure that this is the dean, or named Breckinridge. Maybe the dean is someone else. Maybe I dozed off for a minute or two. I'm perfectly alert and understand exactly what's happening here, it's just that sometimes I doze off for a minute or two. So did Taft.

dean's daughter, Valerie,[2] and the dean doesn't want her hitched to a man chock-full of felonious heredity, even if he *does* look like a brilliant young psychology professor. He doesn't want his grandchildren to "inherit criminal tendencies," as who would? Reagan says pooh, his father was a criminal because he was "born in a slum environment" and couldn't help it.

The dean asks him to resign. He won't. The daughter, Valerie, bounces onto the scene and says not to quarrel with Daddy, they'll just break off their engagement temporarily and everything will be all right.

Back to the lab. Bonzo is on a hunger strike. Hans says maybe he misses his mother. Reagan hugs Bonzo, gives him a bottle, and carries him around humming the Brahms lullaby. Bonzo hums along. Reagan has a brilliant idea for disproving criminal heredity. He will take Bonzo home and "teach this monkey the difference between right and wrong."[3]

Well, you probably know how funny it is when you take a chimpanzee home and put him in pajamas in a crib, and how he takes the pillow apart and fills the room with feathers. Reagan gets on the phone and calls Home Service for a substitute mother for his new baby, and almost before he can hang up, a pretty blonde named Jane comes to the door for the job. There's the usual misunderstanding—Reagan says, "He's a monkey," and Jane says, "They all are," and then when she sees Bonzo she screams "It's a monkey!"[4]

Reagan explains the experiment to her: "Even a monkey

---

[2] *If* that's the dean.

[3] I may have missed the part where they find out *Bonzo's* parents are criminals, unless perhaps all chimpanzees are criminals.

[4] It's not. Monkeys belong to either the *Cercopithecoideae* or the *Ceboideae* and tend to have tails. Chimps are apes and much smarter. They're so smart they can be trained to co-star in movies.

brought up in the right environment can learn the meaning of decency and honesty." Naturally Valerie walks in—fiancées just *never* learn to knock—while Jane's upstairs with Bonzo. There's a long, long scene where Reagan keeps pretending to leave the house and Valerie smells a rat and finally he has to drag her out and duck around and dash back in again.

Jane says Bonzo is much cuter than her brother Gus.

Reagan gets spotted by Professor Fosdick[5] while shopping for baby food. He explains this by saying that he eats the stuff himself to stay young and energetic like a baby.[6] I think there's a reason the whole experiment has to be kept secret, but it got past me somehow.

Cut to breakfast scene, where Bonzo sits in a high chair eating Pablum as a first step to human ethics. Reagan talks a lot of psychology words, like "Oedipus complex" and "aberration." Jane says he isn't acting much like a father. Reagan says, "I guess I have a lot to learn about acting like a father."

They pretend to be married to each other, because this is important for Bonzo's environment. After a couple of weeks even Reagan, who's all thumbs with the ladies, is really getting into this married act, but Valerie's still cutting up. She threatens to come over and visit.

On the two-week anniversary of Bonzo's domestic life, Jane bakes a cake to celebrate, but Reagan doesn't come home. Jane's really nice about it because she's that kind of girl, and tells Bonzo papa's working late at the office. They go to bed. Bonzo has a nightmare and rushes into Jane's bed for comfort. Later, when Reagan comes home, he's delighted because son Bonzo has opened *two* doors to get to

---

[5] Maybe Fosdick is the Dean? No, I guess not.

[6] This might be an important clue for Reaganologists.

his mamma, though actually doorknobs are a cinch compared to eating Pablum with a spoon.[7]

Bonzo steals Jane's beads, and Jane talks him into giving them back to her. This is a landmark, proving that the home-style environment is working on his morals, or that he decided he wasn't the beads type.[8]

Cut to Reagan in classroom, telling his students about conditioned reflexes. Then there's a message for him in the dean's office, in code, saying "Papa's boy is up a tree." Hans cries "Nein!" and he and Reagan rush home.

Bonzo's been on a tear, climbing a tree, ducking through the window to Reagan's office to mess up his desk, and playing with the telephone. The telephone operator, an exceptionally acute one, senses trouble and dispatches police and firemen to Reagan's address. Bonzo bounces back out to the tree. Jane has climbed up after him. Bonzo knocks down her ladder. Reagan and Hans arrive. Branch breaks under Jane. Reagan climbs into tree. Fire trucks arrive. Reagan yells at Jane for letting Bonzo rampage. Police arrive. Valerie arrives. Thinks Bonzo is real child, produced by Reagan and Jane due to Reagan's inherited criminal tendencies, and gives him back his ring. Valerie leaves. Fire trucks leave. Police leave. Reagan wants to give Bonzo back to the lab because the experiment is pointless now that he's not going to marry Valerie. Hans begs him to go on with the project "in the interests of science."

Bonzo is missing again. It's night. Hans and Reagan drive around looking for him. Hans: "How much longer must we search for this noodle in der haystack?" Bonzo turns up gazing into the window of a jewelry store, wrestling with inherited criminal tendencies.

---

[7] Sorry, I forget where he'd been. Out with Valerie, I suppose. No, I was *not* asleep again.

[8] He's a boy chimp, and it's only 1951.

The experiment goes on. Every morning Reagan shows Bonzo how to behave by kissing Jane good-bye, but he's so woolly-headed he still thinks he wants to marry Valerie. He *doesn't even realize* he's in love with Jane, because he's an intellectual and out of touch with his feelings and talks about "Gestalt" and "sublimation" when he ought to just go with the flow.

Re-enter the dean, who has sold Bonzo to Yale for twenty-five hundred dollars for "medical research." Hans says this is no ordinary animal, but "good and kind." This cuts no ice with the dean.

There's a birthday party—Bonzo's, I think—with another cake, and Bonzo shows off his growing humanity by wearing a cowboy suit and riding a tricycle. Jane makes a speech about how it's love that made him like that, because it's love that turns people into human beings, and Hans weeps with Teutonic sentiment.

While she's putting Bonzo to bed, Hans tells Reagan that (a) Bonzo's been sold down the river, and (b) Jane's in love with him.[9]

Reagan knocks on Jane's door, but she's packing and says, "Go away." He goes. Then Bonzo knocks on her door and she says, "I told you to go away." Rejected, he gets on his tricycle and pedals straight to the jewelry store and gets in the back way and heists a fancy necklace from the window.

Reagan gets arrested trying to return the necklace. Jane has finished packing and left. Newspaper headlines: "Jewel Thief." Bonzo crated up for Yale and life in medical research. Reagan in jail. Jane sees headlines and rushes back. She and Hans confess all to Valerie and the dean.[10] Jane tells Bonzo to put the necklace back where he found it, and off he goes, witnesses in hot pursuit. Everyone clusters around

---

[9] No, no, with *Reagan*.

[10] I never did figure out why it was a secret.

store window and sees how he slipped in through a handy vent.

General rejoicing. Reagan exonerated. Cut to celebration. Reagan, now an internationally renowned psychologist for his experiment, "Operation Bonzo," proving environment better than heredity, makes speech. Dean mollified. Valerie mollified. Bonzo excused from Yale. Jane and Reagan get married and drive off in his convertible, with Bonzo hamming it up in the back seat in a cute little suit with suspenders.

Reagan, driving down the boulevard at around forty miles an hour, turns to give Jane a good long kiss, but his luck holds and the car doesn't even swerve. Back at the wheel again, "By golly," he says, "I'm the richest man in six counties!"

THE END

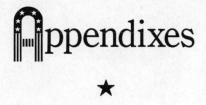

Appendixes

★

Appendix

Appendix I

Martha Washington's Recipe
for Whiskey Cake:

"Take 40 eggs and divide the whites from the yolks and beat them to a froth then work 4 lbs of butter to a cream and put the whites of eggs to it a spoon full at a time till it is well worked then put in the youlks of eggs and 5 lbs of flower and 5 lbs of fruit. 2 hours will bake it add to it half an ounce of mace and nutmeg half a pint of wine and some fresh brandy."

Appendix II

⌒⌒

The Final Draft of the Declaration of Independence, or Everybody's an Editor

When in the course of human events it becomes
necessary for ~~a~~ *one* people to dissolve the political
bonds which have connected them with another,
and to ~~advance from that subordination in which~~
~~they have hitherto remained~~ assume among the
powers of the earth the ~~equal and independent~~ *separate and equal*
station to which the laws of nature & of nature's
god entitle them, a decent respect to the opinions
of mankind requires that they should declare the
causes which impel them to the ~~change.~~ *separation* We hold
these truths to be ~~sacred & undeniable~~ *self-evident* . . .

*("Self-evident" was Franklin's idea. He thought
it was crisper.)*

Appendix III

⁓

From the Checkers Speech

"One other thing I probably should tell you, because if I don't they'll probably be saying this about me too. We did get something, a gift, after the election. A man down in Texas heard Pat on the radio mention the fact that our two youngsters would like to have a dog. And, believe it or not, the day before we left on this campaign trip we got a message from Union Station in Baltimore saying they had a package for us. We went down to get it. You know what it was? It was a little cocker spaniel dog in a crate that he sent all the way from Texas. Black and white spotted. And our little girl Tricia, the six-year-old, named it Checkers. And you know, the kids love the dog, and I just want to say this right now, that regardless of what they say about it, *we're gonna keep it.*"

ABOUT THE AUTHOR

Barbara Holland is an amateur historian, advertising copy-writer, and the author of *Secrets of the Cat*. She lives in Philadel-phia, Pennsylvania.